15.26

San Diego Christian College
2100 Greenfield Drive
El Cajon, CA 92019

784.12
J79m

by

Tom Jones

An Informal Introduction
To The World Of Musical Theatre

LIMELIGHT EDITIONS

First Limelight Edition, January 1998

Copyright © 1998 by Tom Jones

All rights reserved. No part of this book may be reproduced in any form, except by a newspaper or magazine reviewer who wishes to quote brief passages in connection with a review.

Published by Limelight Editions (an imprint of Amadeus Press, LLC)
512 Newark Pompton Turnpike, Pompton Plains, New Jersey 07444, USA
Website: www.limelighteditions.com

Reprinted October 2005

Printed in the United States of America

Library of Congress Cataloging-in-Publication Data

Jones, Tom
Making Musicals
ISBN 0-87910-095-8
1. Musicals—Writing and publishing. 2. Libretto. 3. Lyric writing (Popular music). 4. Musicals—United States—History and criticism. I. Title.
MT67.J775 1997
782.1'4'0973—dc21 97-13033
CIP
MN

For all lyrics: International copyright Secured by Warner Bros. Publications U.S. Inc., Miami, FL 33014

THE DESERT SONG, by Sigmund Romberg, Otto Harbach, Oscar Hammerstein II
© 1926 (Renewed) Chappell & Co.
All Rights Reserved Used by Permission

MUCH MORE, by Tom Jones and Harvey Schmidt
© 1960 (Renewed) Tom Jones and Harvey Schmidt
Chappell & Co. owner of Publication and Allied Rights throughout the World
All Rights Reserved Used by Permission

MY CUP RUNNETH OVER WITH LOVE, by Tom Jones and Harvey Schmidt
© 1966 (Renewed) Tom Jones and Harvey Schmidt
Chappell & Co. owner of Publication and Allied Rights throughout the World
All Rights Reserved Used by Permission

TRY TO REMEMBER, by Tom Jones and Harvey Schmidt
© 1960 (Renewed) Tom Jones and Harvey Schmidt
Chappell & Co. owner of Publication and Allied Rights throughout the World
All Rights Reserved Used by Permission

WITHIN THIS EMPTY SPACE, by Tom Jones and Harvey Schmidt
© Tom Jones and Harvey Schmidt (Copyright Renewed)
Chappell & Co. owner of Publication and Allied Rights throughout the World
All Rights Reserved Used by Permission

Photos © Museum of the City of New York. Used by permission.

American Music Hall Vaudeville Bill, August 23, 1909
Ziegfeld Follies, 1926
Naughty Marietta, 1910
Advertising Postcard for *The Desert Song* at the Casino Theatre, 1926
Princess Theatre interior, view from the Proscenium
Very Good Eddie, 1915 (Gift of F. Ray Comstock)
Nell Brinkley: Impressions of Ziegfeld's *Show Boat*, 1927
On Your Toes, 1936 (Photo: White Studio)
Scene from *West Side Story*, 1957 (Photo: Friedman-Abeles)
Early Sketch of *Follies* basic set, 1971
Scene from *Hair*, 1967

All other illustrations are from the private collection of the author.

For

Harvey Schmidt

Contents

Foreword

Based on a series of lectures I gave at Hunter College in New York, this book is intended as a general introduction to the world of musical theatre, with a little autobiography and general "schmoozing" thrown in for good measure.

The first half deals, in broad and general terms, with the growth and development of the American musical, how it evolved through a curious mixture of "variety" entertainment and European operetta to become one of the distinctive native art forms created in this country.

The second half deals with the practical "how-to" of putting together a musical, using my own career and the shows I have worked on as a springboard to examine the form in general.

My purpose here is to give general information to the interested layman, plus a few "tricks of the trade" to anyone wishing to go further and try writing for the musical stage.

Introduction

Let me begin by telling you who I am—where I come from, and what my beliefs and aspirations are.

I studied Drama at the University of Texas. I was there six years, from 1945 through 1951, obtaining undergraduate and graduate degrees in the field of Play Directing (or "Production," as it was rather mysteriously called).

The U. T. Drama Department was a wonderful one, full of extraordinary professors and talented students, many of whom have gone on to successful careers in theatre and film. We did literally hundreds of plays during my stay there, everything from Aeschylus to Shakespeare to Shaw to the emerging Tennessee Williams.

But we never did a musical. Not one. Not even an operetta. Not even Gilbert and Sullivan. Musicals were considered too "frivolous," too "lightweight." They were beneath our consideration. In short, they were forbidden fruit. And they were irresistible.

There existed on the campus an organization called the Curtain Club, an extra-curricular group which had been formed early in the century by the noted theatre critic and essayist Stark Young to provide a place for students who wished to put on plays and skits on their own. It was here, under this umbrella, that we escaped from our awesome agenda into the world of "show-biz," grinding out weekly songs and dances, topped off, in due course, by the annual "College Musical."

Ah, the college musical. You know what it is. Or perhaps you don't know. At least, you don't know what it was. Nowadays, if it exists at all, it tends to be a complex contemporary opera in the style of Sondheim, filled with intricate rhythms and blistering irony.

Then, it was pure fun. Razz-ma-tazz. Comedy songs and lovesick ballads and bump and grind and tap-dance, and occasional scenic breakthroughs like having a girl sing a torchsong while standing underneath a lamppost. Things that we saw in the movies. Things that we imagined while listening for endless hours to that sensational new invention, the Broadway original cast album.

Here, from my first college musical, is a song with music and lyrics by Harvey L. Schmidt, full-time art student and part-time pianist for the Curtain Club. The show was a revue called *Hipsy-Boo!* Our director, Word Baker, who was then still known as Charlie, had the crew build a runway out around the orchestra pit and arranged to give away free tickets to bald-headed men who sat in the first row. Then, with the glow of spotlights reflecting off their expectant domes, Mr. Schmidt sat at the piano, started the racky-tacky downbeat, and eight succulent young Texas damsels wearing mesh stocking and colorful garters (and little else) pranced out onto the runway and sang:

> Hello, Fellas,
> We're here to greet you
> With a song and a smile:
> Dance all the while.
>
> Hello, Boys,
> We hope that you like a show
> With girlies and gags:
> Music that rags.

You'll find that we're pals in the end
And we will always be true-blue.
We're the pride of this th-e-atre.
Show your dough and see more later.
Hope our kicks do something for you.

Because we L (Bump)
O (Bump) VE,
Love you, Boys.
And hope you're here to stay.

Hope that you won't
(Bump)
Stray too far away
Cause racky-tacky-ticky-too:
We love men with eyes of blue.

So glad your wife's at home crocheting
While you're sashaying
Round town!

For it's: One! Two!
Doin' the Hipsy-Boo!
Three-Four, Honey,
Ya know what it does to you.

Goodbye, Boys,
We're glad to have welcomed you.
Doin' that old One-Two!
Givin' a kick for you!
Doin' the Hipsy-Boo
Rag!

That's all for now, Boys,
And goodbye to you.

> We hope that you've enjoyed our little
> Hipsy-Boo!

I need hardly tell you that this show was a smash. It was more than that. It was epochal. It was, for us, the sort of hit that *South Pacific* was for Rodgers and Hammerstein on Broadway. The two-week run was sold out instantly. There was ticket scalping (a first for the University of Texas). Students shaved their heads in the hope of getting one of the free seats in the first row.

I, who had written the comedy sketches, was awestruck. This was different. Different than what we had been doing in the Department of Drama. It was different, not only in its extreme success, but it was different in the kind of basic theatrical *experience*.

This was hotter, somehow. It was more immediate. It placed the audience and the actors in a different relationship, a new kind of give-and-take.

Later that school year, I was offered the opportunity to direct the other big annual campus musical, the one for the big auditorium. (Our *Hipsy-Boo!* hit had been more or less "Off-Broadway," a revue in a 499-seat house in an army surplus recreation hall.)

Since the directing assignment paid a fee, I eagerly accepted the offer. But when I read the various scripts and heard the songs being submitted by prospective writers, I quickly came to the conclusion that I could do it better myself. Rather, I could do it better by myself, with someone else. I had no illusions then, nor do I now, that I could ever compose a piece of music. So, thinking back to that *Hipsy-Boo!* song, I sought out Harvey Schmidt and asked him if he would like to do the music for an original musical, with me doing book and lyrics.

No sooner had he said yes than we were off and running (off and writing). And six weeks later, we opened our brand new original college musical with a complete score by Jones and Schmidt. It was, if anything, even more successful than *Hipsy-Boo!* I won't bore you with the details, even though now, many decades later, I still get pleasure from remembering the pleasure that this show provided to us and to the fifteen hundred souls who were lucky enough to fight their way into the auditorium each night.

Then it was over. Or so we thought. I graduated, was drafted, and went into the army. Harvey graduated a year later and did the same. (This was during the Korean War.) We went our separate ways, with me dreaming of becoming a director and Harvey dreaming of becoming a commercial artist.

Even so, there was something. Some little something. Perhaps it was that still dimly resonating sound of laughter and yes, cliché though it is, applause. There was something that made us keep in touch, that made me send him new lyrics through the mail, that made him send me music on those old 78 rpm records which he cut at a local sound studio near his army camp.

I have never been able to sing. Not really. I have always been embarrassed to try. But something about writing songs and having people sing them, and having them come to life—there was something in that which answered a deep need in me. Though I did not know it, I was already "hooked."

Then, there was something else as well.

Before I finished my college education, I came gradually to realize that there were two kinds of theatre: one that I liked, and one that I didn't like as much.

The kind that I liked was what might be called "presentational" theatre, "poetic" theatre, the theatre of Shakespeare and the Greeks and Thornton Wilder and Bertold Brecht.

The kind that I didn't like as much was what might be called "realistic" theatre, "prose" theatre, the theatre which almost totally dominated the stage for the first half of the twentieth century.

I didn't like stage sets very much. That is, I didn't like "realistic" stage sets—sets which purported to be the actual environments where the action took place. I didn't like living room walls and charming bric-a-brac and pretend windows with pretend bushes outside. Something in me resisted the whole thing, as if someone were trying to trick me. I felt the urge to say: "Come on, who are you kidding? I know that's not a real door. I know that the tree outside is made of papier-mâché and held up by a stage brace."

On the other hand, if little or no pretense was made to literally depict a place, I had no trouble in believing in its reality. A suggestion was all I needed, all I wanted. Any more than that took away the fun, the magic, the creation. It robbed me as an audience member of my part in the proceedings. It limited my imagination. The whole thing was a paradox: Try to convince me that it was really real and I resisted. Admit to me that it was false and I could believe in its reality.

Also, and in a similar way, I didn't like plays where the actors spent all of their time just talking to each other and never acknowledged the presence of the audience. It seemed stupid to me. And rude. And again, it robbed the experience of the direct involvement and participation of the audience.

Thinking about this over a long period of time, I came gradually to understand what it was about this presentational theatre that I liked so much. There are four things:

1. Fluidity of form.

Because there is no cumbersome realistic scenery, you can go anywhere you want. You are free to skip over time and place in a flowing nonstop way. All that is necessary are a few (well-chosen) words.

2. Linguistic magic.

Not being literally realistic, the characters (and thus the writer) are free to speak in a language that is more colorful and dynamic and full of nuance and variation than ordinary speech. Thus, the music and the magic that lie locked inside our language are free to be released, and the words themselves can do more than just convey a character's thoughts and emotions; they can help produce emotion on their own, in exactly the same way that sounds and rhythms and "melodies" can produce emotion in music.

Why should there be a theatre, after all? We live in a world of moving pictures and radio and television. Realistic drama is much better served by film and TV than by theatre. With a close-up, you can get close. There can be very realistic speech. There is no need to "project," no need to write lines that sing—or soar. No need to write "lines" at all. A turn of the head, a look in the eyes, that will do it. It is "subtext" which counts, not text. Image which counts, not words.

And what about melodrama and spectacle, those other mainstays of nineteenth-century drama? They are much more effective on a screen. The chase, the daring escape, the girl tied to the railroad track—these absolute staples of popular entertainment simply moved headquarters to Hollywood. If they were big spectacles (like *Ben Hur*, a perennial favorite on stage at one time), they transferred themselves to the movies. If they were simply hold-your-breath will-the-hero-be-saved melodramas, they became the backbone of television programming, along with the pleasant domestic comedies, the "sitcoms" which provided so much of the Broadway stage fare until the small screen done 'em in.

So, why have a theatre at all? What can it provide that the others cannot? The answer, I think, has something to do with the group experience and the spoken word.

The theatre, after all, is surely one of the last bastions of the spoken word. In an increasingly visual world, the theatre provides a place where people may gather and have a group experience induced primarily by the power of words. And, surprisingly, these needs are still deep within us. They will not be dropped so quickly. They are part of us, part of our species. To gather in a circle and have a story told, to experience a group reaction (possibly even a group revelation)—this is a basic need. Too bad the theatre nowadays so often forgets that.

3. Theatrical Conventions.

Not being "realistic," the kind of theatre that I like can have all manner of useful theatrical conventions, such as:

Direct address to the audience.

A Narrator, if desired, to speed us through time and space.

Soliloquies. Spoken arias.

The free use of music and dance.

4. Schmaltz.

Not being literally "realistic," this kind of theatre can dare to be outrageously theatrical. Take Shakespeare, for example. No one has ever been more outrageously theatrical than Shakespeare. When Lear goes mad, the whole world erupts in a howling storm. When Gloucester is blind to which of his sons is the true one, Regan's husband, Cornwall, gouges his eye out on-stage: "Out, vile jelly!" And out it pops. Lady Macbeth, sleepwalking, tries over and over to wipe the guilty blood off her hands. But she cannot do it: "All the perfumes of Arabia will not sweeten this little hand." And this speech in itself is an echoing of Macbeth's: "Will all great Neptune's ocean wash this blood clean from my hand? No, this my hand will rather the multitudinous seas incarnadine, making the green one red." This is like opera. Like Sophocles. This is bigger than life, larger than the confines of realism.

So, these are the elements of great theatre, as I perceive them: fluidity of form, linguistic magic, presentational conventions, and sheer dramatic schmaltz.

Looking around me, I gradually came to realize that the one place where all of these presentational forms were accepted in a natural way in my own time was in the musical theatre. The heightened language, the fluidity, the theatricality, the direct address—all of these were the stock and staple of the musical stage.

I must admit that the situation has changed a bit since I came to this conclusion so many years ago. The "straight" play, which totally dominated the stage at that time, has become less "straight." Influenced perhaps by musical theatre, many plays now make use, good use, of these presentational forms; the audience accepts *M Butterfly* or *Angels in America* with pleasure for the very same reasons it has long relished musicals.

To make a long story short, I decided that the American musical offered a wonderful opportunity to pursue the kind of theatre that I felt in my bones was the real theatre, the theatre which answered that deep need in myself and others. And those roars of laughter and applause still echoed in my head from our college musical days.

A popular theatre. Yes, that's what I wanted. A popular theatre with the potential to become a holy theatre as well. And I thought: as long as you can have all this, as well as dancing and singing, and the opportunity to work with beautiful and talented men and women, what more could you ask?

And I resolved to spend my life in the musical theatre.

Part One:

A Brief History of the American Musical

1

VARIETY

There is nothing new about the musical theatre. It is very old, as old as the theatre itself. Although we have scant knowledge of the "theatre" of primitive man, we have only to look at present-day survivors of aboriginal cultures to realize that the theatre began with drumming and with chants and with body decoration and with dance. And with enactments of a ritual, a ritual of magic.

All down through history, beginning with the ancient Greeks, through the Middle Ages and the Renaissance, through the oratorios, the early operas, the court masques, the inserted songs and dances (à la Shakespeare) right on up through the ballad operas and the operettas, the pasticcios and the pantomimes and the burlettas, the stage has always been alive with the sound of music.

However, though musical theatre itself is old, what is new, or relatively new, is the "American musical." Though of course it is umbilically connected to its origins in western Europe, it is still considered distinctive enough to be classed, along with jazz, as a uniquely American contribution to the arts. It is the "American" musical—whether written by Americans or Europeans—that the rest of the world is eager to embrace. From Tokyo to Berlin, the most popular form of theatrical endeavor today is the American musical.

While there were many influences and much cross pollination in the development of the American musical, it is my belief that there were two primary sources whose influence exceeded all others. These two sources were Variety and Operetta.

The Minstrel Show

The origins of the variety show in this country stem more or less directly from the minstrel show. In America, Negro caricatures in song and dance and comedy routines were frequently used between acts of regular shows in the eighteenth century. The first really popular and well-known blackface *act* was devised by Thomas Rice, who in the first half of the nineteenth century borrowed Negro clothes and sang and danced a number called "Jim Crow." (Oh, ominous beginning!)

This was followed in time by blackface groups, the most famous of which was the Virginia Minstrels, opened by Dan Emmett in 1843. This group set the format and established the style of the early minstrels, and Dan Emmett wrote most of the songs, some of which, like "Blue Tail Fly" and "Polly Wolly Doodle" are still popular today, a hundred and fifty years later.

The style for the later minstrel shows, and, indeed, the style that became *the* minstrel show, was devised by Edward Christy with his famous Christy's Minstrels.

It was he who sat the minstrels in a semicircle around the stage, with an Interlocutor in the middle and two "End Men" at either side. He introduced and perfected the three-act minstrel show format. Act One presented variety entertainment. Act Two was known as the "Fantasia." Act

Three was a parody or burlesque.

Minstrel shows were popular. Overwhelmingly so. In the nineteenth century, Christy's Minstrels, charging 25 cents admission, grossed 317,598 dollars for a single run of a minstrel program.* If we upped that by ten times, to the cost of $2.50 per ticket, that would be 3 million, 175 thousand, 980 dollars. If we upped it one hundred times, to a ticket price of 25 dollars, it would be 31 million, 759 thousand, 800 dollars. And if you doubled that, bringing it to a top ticket price of 50 dollars, the gross would be 63 million, 519 thousand, and 600 dollars. (Eat your heart out, Cameron Mackintosh.)

After their huge success throughout the nineteenth century, minstrel shows finally began their decline. The ingredients that had made up the minstrels regrouped themselves and became something new. The variety act of the minstrels grew into *vaudeville*. The parodies turned into *revue*. The low comedy and stock ethnic types became *burlesque*. And these three things, different though they seemed, had one major trait in common: they were, essentially, the art of the "put-together"—the "bill."

Vaudeville

American vaudeville began right after the Civil War when a former minstrel showman named Tony Pastor opened a theater for variety entertainment in Paterson, New Jersey. He took the variety routines, threw out the blackface and the semicircle, and concentrated on family entertainment. No drinking. No smoking. No vulgarity. A place where you could bring the wife and kids.

When Tony Pastor's career began to fade, E. F. Albee continued the policy of clean, family entertainment. So did

**The Musical* by Richard Kislan, Prentice-Hall, 1980.

The "put-together" of the bill became one of the basic forces that formed the American musical.

AMERICAN MUSIC HALL

AND ROOF GARDENS
Storm-Proof and Star lit

42d Street
West of Broadway

Smoking in all parts
of the Theatre

WILLIAM MORRIS, Inc. New York, London, Chicago Lessees & Managers

NOTE—This theatre is one of the chain of Independent Vaudeville Houses under the direction of William Morris, Inc., embracing the principal cities of the United States. There will be presented with weekly change of bill the best vaudeville acts of America and Europe.

Week Beginning Monday Matinee, Aug. 23, 1909
DAILY MATINEE DOWNSTAIRS

1 **OVERTURE**
Musical Director....... ....Louis Berlinghoff

2 **THE PICAGY TRIO**
Acrobatic Marvels

3 **INA CLAIR**
Singing Comedienne and Impersonations

Coming "DIVINE MYRMA" Coming

Second Successful Week
"The King of Diamonds"
4 **HERBERT LLOYD**
Burlesque on Vaudeville

The American Soprano
5 **MABEL McKINLEY**
Singing a Number of Her Own and Popular Selections

The Terpsichorean Sensation of the Season
6 **John C. Smith and Ethel Donaldson**
In their Own Original Conception of the "Vampire Dance"
Founded on Kipling's Famous Title of the Same Name

The Two Comedians
7 **AL. FIELDS and DAVE LEWIS**
Creators and Producers of Everything they do
In a Comedy Skit "The Misery of a Hansom Cab"

Coming "DIVINE MYRMA" Coming

Continued Triumph of
8 **MAURICE LEVI AND HIS ALL STAR BAND**
Note.—This is Mr. Levi's first appearance in vaudeville since his remarkable engagement at Manhattan Beach. At this famous seaside resort of Coney Island, he has entertained more than a million people. He will also offer for the first time his greatest composition, "The March of the United States," representing the presentation of a battleship by each State in the Union to "Uncle Sam," making it the greatest navy in the world. (All Rights Reserved).

INTERMISSION

LAST WEEK LAST WEEK
Farewell to New York
THE MORE MAN THAN MONKEY
9 **CONSUL, THE GREAT**
MANY IMITATE—NONE COMPARE
(Consul's Costumes by Max Marx)

Last Engagement in Vaudeville of 'The Cheeriest Comedienne'
10 **STELLA MAYHEW**
London's American Favorite with Billee Taylor

Coming "DIVINE MYRMA" Coming

First Time Here
11 **DE WITT YOUNG AND SISTER**
The College Boy Juggler and The Lady Boomerang Thrower

12 **AMERISCOPE**

Coming "DIVINE MYRMA" Coming

Keith, and a number of others. Vaudeville continued to prosper. Theater after dazzling theater was built, each one more opulent than the last. Circuits were established, great "wheels" of theatres booked by one major impresario. An actor or actress, a variety performer, or sometimes a whole family of performers, could get bookings that filled up the entire year.

In the early part of this century there were nearly two thousand theatres across America featuring weekly programs of nine acts on the bill. In addition to the singers and dancers and comedians, there were magicians and acrobats and animal acts and Swiss bell ringers and fire eaters and female impersonators and occasional appearances by internationally famous stars such as Sarah Bernhardt, who performed her famous love scenes in French and who toured American vaudeville for years, even after she had one wooden leg. Famous people who had just been in the news such as boxers or baseball stars appeared on vaudeville stages for the public to see "in person." For those of you old enough to remember, just think of the Ed Sullivan show and multiply it by two thousand.

As time went on, the programming and sequence of the bill became a highly developed art. As any of you know who have ever tried to put together a revue or a variety show, the sequencing is just as important as the material itself.

This issue of sequencing was very important to the development of musical theatre in America. The "put-together" became more important than the acts themselves. And the person, whoever he might be—producer, author, composer, or director—who had the final say about put-together was the person who ultimately determined the success or failure (both artistically and commercially) of the show.

Vaudeville grew and prospered, as the minstrel shows had done before, and then it too declined until finally *Va-*

riety the show business bible, took "Variety" off the front page and stuck it at the back (where "Legit" now precipitously resides). For a while the big movie palaces ran a few variety bills between showings, but this soon proved unnecessary. The public had no great desire to see living human beings, especially if they could see Clark Gable and Bette Davis in close-ups fifty feet high.

Burlesque

The American burlesque tradition also began in the latter part of the nineteenth century. It involved "extravaganzas" mixing spectacle, comedy, and dainty ladies. ("Dainty" weighing in at 180 pounds or so.) The early shows generally followed much the same format as the minstrel, with one major difference: women were part of the cast. In some instances there might be the added attraction of a "hootchy-kootchy" dance or, alternately, an elaborate finale featuring a number of semi-clothed ladies in *tableaux-vivant*. But for the most part the shows were relatively clean, featuring low comics who did "burlesque" or "low comedy" routines using "Dutch" or Yiddish dialect and lots of physical "slapstick" gags. (The connections with *commedia dell'arte* and, beyond that, to ancient Roman comedy are particularly striking—no pun intended.)

At some point in the development of the form, some ladies took their pants off. According to *Variety*, it was just before the First World War that the western "wheel" began giving dirty shows. According to others, the "strip-tease" began at Minsky's. Wherever it was, it signaled the beginning of the end of the burlesque form when the naked ladies became more important than the brilliant comedians. After all, anyone can bump and grind and take their clothes off, but a true comedian is a work of art. Whereas works of art can find devoted and loyal patrons, strippers rarely build an audience that you can count on to come back time and time again.

Revue

The thing that distinguishes revue and makes it different from vaudeville is the theme, for in revue there is a single idea or concept that unifies the whole show and ties it together.

The theme of the *Ziegfeld Follies* was to "glorify the American girl" often in exotic settings as pictured above.

For example, the theme of the Ziegfeld Follies was to "glorify the American girl." The theme of Leonard Sillman's many revues was to introduce "new faces." The theme of the thirties hit *Pins and Needles* was to glorify (and spoof) the unions, using real workers from the Ladies' Garment Worker's Union as cast members. Ben Bagley's revues were intended to introduce new writers; Julius Monk's to spoof and celebrate New York City in sophisticated terms. And recently, the theme of the successful *Forbidden Broadway* series is to make fun of the current theatrical season.

Revues have traditionally taken two basic forms: big and small. The big ones, like the *Follies* and the *Vanities*, had plenty of pulchritude, lavish sets, and costumes as well as famous variety stars like Fanny Brice and Will Rogers. The small ones rejected glamour and spectacle in favor of clever, sophisticated writing and bright new performers. This sort of intimate revue continued right up to our own time (at least, right up to my own time). In the intervening years, Irving Berlin, Cole Porter, George Gershwin, Harold Rome, and Comden and Green all wrote extensively for the revue format. And within recent memory, there were many young writers who first had their work done in New York in revues. Among them are Sheldon Harnick, Mary Rodgers, Jerry Herman, Cy Coleman, Lee Adams and Charles Strouse, Stephen Sondheim, and Tom Jones and Harvey Schmidt.

In Conclusion

Beginning with the minstrel shows and branching out into vaudeville, burlesque and revue, the American musical was begat in large part by "variety," by star turns and comedy routines and spectacle and "put-together." Indeed, many of the most successful variety performers began to expand into the "legitimate" theatre.

The comedy team of Weber and Fields took their "Dutch" comic routines from burlesque and turned them into "book shows." Based on the old minstrel formula, they took their stock characters and placed them in a variety of exotic locales or in a send-up of some famous play or story. The characters they played never changed, no matter what the time or place. Neither did the comedy. Their jokes were as old as Athens, as new as the latest American immigration. Physical comedy, "slapstick," was always there, plus the exaggerated

German accents.

As Weber and Fields did with German (or "Dutch," as it was called) immigration, so Harridan and Hart did with the Irish. They took their comic characters and routines from vaudeville and turned them into a series of shows based upon the "Mulligan Guard." In the same style, but even more successful, was that quintessential Broadway type, George M. Cohan. He too came from vaudeville. He was born into it, really; part of a family act. And in addition to bringing the skills and traditions of vaudeville into the theatre, he also brought his enormous talents as a writer of catchy, singable songs.

In most of these early Broadway musicals, the books were minimal. Song writers mattered. So did stars. Book-writers did not. Even today, the book-writer of a musical is almost always considered the last in the pecking order. Ask anyone you know who wrote *The Sound of Music*, *Fiddler on the Roof* or *Sweeney Todd* and you will see what I mean.

2

OPERETTAS

As you have probably noticed, in real life things are not quite as neat and sub-paragraphed as they are in history books or lectures on musical theatre. In fact, many categories of musical entertainment were happening at the same time, constantly cross-pollinating and influencing each other.

The Black Crook opened in 1866, the first American "musical" (in quotes), with a plot and songs and a huge (in more ways than one) chorus of female dancers in tights. It opened at Niblo's Garden in New York, was a monster hit, and was followed in a couple of years by *Evangeline,* actually billed as a "musical comedy," with a score composed especially for the show, which was not the case with *The Black Crook*. There were others, most notably Charles Hoyt's *A Trip to Chinatown* in 1880. But these musical shows were sporadic and unrelated and not part of an ongoing movement or trend.

Of the influences on the book musical, the most important models came from abroad.

First, there was the opéra bouffe, particularly those of Jacques Offenbach, whose witty, somewhat naughty, productions were popular in the United States even though the shows were performed in French. The English outgrowths of these French works, particularly Gilbert and Sullivan, were even more popular. The tunes were just as lively and as lovely (though perhaps without that melancholy strain). The stories were just as comic, the endings as happy, and they were in English. And not just in any English, but the best and wittiest English ever written in lyric form.

The U. S. premiere of *H.M.S. Pinafore* in 1878 created a sensation. Within a year, more than ninety *Pinafore* companies were touring the country, all of them successful, none of them paying royalties. There was no reciprocal copyright agreement at the time and anyone could simply appropriate the material, put together a production, hang up a sign, and start selling tickets. It was for that reason that Gilbert and Sullivan decided to open their next musical, *The Pirates of Penzance*, in America rather than in England. At least that way they could draw royalties from the initial production before the wave of theatrical piracy got under way.

The Gilbert and Sullivan operettas that followed were not as incredibly popular in the United States as *Pinafore* had been, but were still popular enough to be around over a century later, having productions and doing business and garnering new fans. And there is scarcely a lyricist worth his salt who did not become intrigued with lyric writing after falling in love with Mr. Gilbert's verses. But however important Gilbert was to prospective lyricists, the truth of the matter is that the European operetta had much more of an influence on the American musical than comic opera or opéra bouffe.

The operetta form was developed in Germany and Austria during the latter part of the nineteenth century. The ingredients were similar to those of the comic opera, but the tone was different, for here the emphasis was upon romance, and the comedy, though still important, was subordinate to adventure, color, music, swashbuckling, and Love with a capital L. An elegant confection, not too nutritious perhaps, but delicious to the taste, like a fine Viennese pastry.

The successes of the genre were mainly variations on a theme. They were all in three acts. They were all about the nobility and the privileged classes (with a few gypsies thrown in). They all had elaborate plots. They all depended upon the music for their success rather than on the book or the lyrics. All required trained singers. And they were all hugely popular—in Vienna, in Europe, in London, and in the United States.

Following the models of these European operettas, the Americans began to create operettas of their own. There were three men who were primarily responsible for the success of the American operetta form. Naturally, all three were composers rather than lyricists or librettists. All three were born and trained in Europe, but all three achieved their fame in America.

The first was Victor Herbert. Born in Ireland and brought up in Stuttgart and Vienna, he studied musical composition and played the cello (which, interestingly enough, was Offenbach's instrument as well). He married an opera singer, who managed to bring him along for the orchestra when she was hired to appear at the Met. In America he prospered, first as musical director of the New York National Guard band and then as a composer. His first big hit was *The Wizard of the Nile* in 1895.

Notice the setting. Exotic Egypt. Whereas most of the Viennese operettas were contemporary and set in middle Europe, most of the American operettas were set either in the past or in some exotic locale. Victor Herbert set operettas in India, Afghanistan, Persia, early France, Germany, and Venice. One of his greatest successes, *Naughty Marietta*, was indeed set in America, but it was an imaginary America of an earlier, more romantic time. Let's look at its history.

Oscar Hammerstein, grandfather of the famous Oscar Hammerstein of our time, was a theatrical producer who loved opera. He built an opera house in New York and maintained a complete opera company in competition with the Metropolitan. Around 1910, mounting debts finally forced him to make a deal with the Met which stipulated that for a certain sum of money he would give up his opera venture and stop the competition. However, this left him with a theatre, an orchestra, and a company, headed by a diminutive (and expensive) soprano named Emma Trintini.

What to do? What else? Get Victor Herbert on the phone. Get an original libretto by Rida Johnson Young. (Who?) Call the whole thing *Naughty Marietta*, open it on Broadway, and run for two smash years.

The plot? Well, yes. Let's see. The French colony in New Orleans in the eighteenth century. The son of the governor of the colony is actually the dread pirate Bras Prique. A group of woodsmen arrive in town ("Tramp. Tramp. Tramp. The boys are marching.") Their leader is Dick Warrington, accompanied by his comic (of course) sidekick.

A "bride-ship" has just arrived from France with young ladies destined to wed colonists. Among them is one "Naughty Marietta," who runs away rather than be married by decree. She is first seen (heard) singing "Ah, Sweet Mystery Of Life." And, winning the friendship of Captain Dick, she accompanies him disguised as a boy and eventually gets a job in a marionette theatre.

After a number of plot complications, the Governor's son is exposed as the dastardly pirate that he is, Marietta marries Captain Dick (after first singing "I'm Falling In Love With Someone") and all ends happily, and successfully. The show was a hit.

The world of operetta: gypsies, pirates, mounties—manly men and womanly women.
(From *Naughty Marietta*)

On the closing night, Victor Herbert himself conducted the orchestra, and when Emma Trintini sang her big number, "The Italian Street Song" ("Zing, zing, zing-a-zing-zing, zing boom bah!"), the crowd went wild, almost tearing the house down with their applause and cheers. However, when she refused, despite Victor Herbert's insistence, to come back out for an encore, Herbert left the pit in a pique and told Hammerstein he would never work for him (or with Emma) again.

What could be done? *Naughty Marietta* was closing. Emma Trintini was already scheduled to appear the following season in a new musical called *The Firefly*, to be produced by Hammerstein's son Arthur with a score by Victor Herbert. A new composer had to be found right away.

At the suggestion of Max Dreyfus of Harms's Music (and later of Chappell), Arthur decided to trust the music to a new composer named Rudolf Friml. The choice was a wise one. Friml completed the score in a month, working with a new librettist named Otto Hauerback (later Harbach). And the Hammerstein dynasty had their second huge hit in a row.

Let me pause for a moment and tell you of my own brief encounter with Max Dreyfus, who signed Harvey and me with Chappell Music in 1960.

We were taken to Chappell by Max Gordon, the veteran Broadway producer who had done many shows, ranging from plays like *Born Yesterday* to musicals like *Roberta*. Max, though seventy-five years old at the time, was looked on by the top men at Chappell (who were in their nineties) as "the kid." Well, somehow "the kid" had heard some of our songs, and he loved them; he became our champion, arranging for us to go up to Chappell and audition for Max Dreyfus himself.

At the appointed hour we were led into an impressive suite of rooms in Rockefeller Center. In the middle was a huge concert grand piano. Over to the side, spread out indiscriminately, were three or four "Barca Loungers," huge reclining leather chairs. And atop each chair was an ancient man dozing peacefully. We were immensely relieved when the door opened and Max Dreyfus, wide awake and wily, was ushered into the room and over to his place by the curve of the grand piano.

Then Harvey played and we both sang. We sang and sang, pulling out everything we could think of from our still modest trunk. Not a word was said. Not a sign was given. There was no sound except for our voices and the piano and the occasional deep rumble of a snore from the lounge department. After thirty minutes or so, Max Dreyfus gave a signal, and all of the lesser minions who were assembled around the outskirts of the room leapt forward and assisted him to the exit. He mumbled something on his way out, but it was so distant that none of us could hear. Finally, Max Gordon had the temerity to shout: "What? What did he say?" And Dreyfus, at the doorway, turned just long enough to repeat "Sign 'em" before he shuffled on out.

And that was all. We were signed with Chappell. We were part of the Establishment. It wouldn't mean much today, but consider the time and place. Max Dreyfus was not only the publisher of Cole Porter and Jule Styne and Leonard Bernstein and Stephen Sondheim, he had also helped move Jerry Kern up from rehearsal pianist to composer. He had done the same for Rudolf Friml. He had guided Gershwin along from the time he was a song-plugger. He had launched Rodgers and Hart. He had been the publisher for Rodgers and Hammerstein. He was part of the living heritage of the American musical theatre, a man whose whole life had been spent nurturing and developing the great talents of Broadway.

Back in the world of operetta, Rudolph Friml remained active on Broadway for many years, often working with Otto Harbach, often being produced by Arthur Hammerstein, and eventually working with Hammerstein's nephew, Oscar. Friml was a veritable fountain of melodic inspiration. He composed all of the time. He believed, along with Herbert, that the music was all. The libretto was there to serve the music. So were the lyrics. He was of the old school. The new ideas of integration and character development were beyond him. One of his biggest successes was *The Vagabond King*. His last hit was *The Three Musketeers* in 1928. In the 1960's, when Harvey and I joined with Chappell Music, we would see him sometimes, at the great concert piano, still composing, still dreaming of another smash.

Sigmund Romberg was different. Although he too was a product of a European background and wrote in the European operetta mold, he did value the book. He refused to write a note of music until the book was finished. He looked for his inspiration in the story.

Of course, this is all relative. He still created within the operetta traditions, but his attitude towards the libretto reflected the wave of the future. Whereas Friml's last hit came in 1928, Romberg's last hits were *Up in Central Park* done in 1945, and *The Girl in the Pink Tights*, produced after his death, in 1953.

Romberg came to the United States soon after the turn of the century, sent by his Hungarian parents in an attempt to distract him from a career in music. The plan didn't work. He got a job playing in an orchestra and began writing some dance tunes. In 1914 he was hired to write songs for the Shubert Brothers, who owned theaters and produced shows in whatever style happened to be popular at the moment. As "staff composer," Romberg worked on fourteen musicals in twenty-six months. Finally one of these shows, *May-Time*, became a big hit and helped establish his reputation.

He left the Shuberts and began producing or co-producing his own shows. He contributed songs to *Poor Little Ritz Girl* to supplement a score written by the new team of Rodgers and Hart. He teamed with the Shuberts again (and with Schubert) on *Blossom Time*. He wrote *Bombo* for Al Jolson, and, working with Otto Harbach and Oscar Hammerstein, he wrote one of his greatest hits, *The Desert Song*.

For a long while Sigmund Romberg went out of fashion. Then after Rodgers and Hammerstein (and all that implies), he scored again (no pun intended) with *Up In Central Park*, a 1945 operetta in the R & H mold. He died in 1951 while working on *The Girl in Pink Tights*, which opened in late 1953 and ran into 1954.

In summation, these were the Big Three of the American operetta: Victor Herbert, Rudolph Friml, Sigmund Romberg. They reigned supreme from the 1890's through the 1920's. They were European in background, European in feeling. Even with occasional American settings, the scores still smacked (delightfully) of old Vienna. Beginning with Victor Herbert, the shows were in two acts (a definite improvement over their European counterparts). The settings were elaborate and often spectacular. The music was more important than lyrics, and both were more important than the book. Trained voices were required. The librettos were frequently based upon other sources.

It was make-believe, a fairy tale: gypsies, pirates, mounties, manly men and womanly women. And though the popularity of operettas waned somewhere around 1930, their influence continued to be felt for generations.

They are the second of the two mainstreams of the American musical.

3

The Third Influence: Jerome Kern

As the two mainstreams, Variety and Operetta, continued surging forward, moving towards the later fusion which would form the authentic "American musical," there was a third influence evolving at more or less the same time. This influence, which, for want of a more generic term, I will simply call the "Princess shows," was strongly influenced by the London stage and its hero and champion was Jerome Kern.

In 1914 a sixteen-year-old George Gershwin, attending his aunt's wedding, heard the orchestra play a song from the new Jerome Kern musical, *The Laughing Husband.* The young composer was so impressed that he resolved to study Kern's music and learn from his style. Two years later, a fourteen-year-old Richard Rodgers went to see Jerome Kern's *Very Good Eddie* over and over again, trying to get a feel for the style of the musical numbers.

What they were responding to was something new, a new kind of approach to musical theatre and to the writing of songs. Many years later, Alan Jay Lerner said that Kern was the pioneer, the one who showed the way. And he didn't mean just the way with the music, he meant the way with the whole show, for Kern was one of the very first to come up with the idea of the integrated musical.

Let us pause for a minute and take a look at two songs. One is from *The Desert Song*: music by Rudolf Friml, lyrics by Oscar Hammerstein II. It opened November, 1926, but the style could just as easily have been from 1916 or 1906, or even 1896. It is a love song and it is called, like the show's title, "The Desert Song."

The other song we want to look at is from a show called *The Girl From Utah*, a British import of 1914 (twelve years earlier than "The Desert Song"), in which the young Jerome Kern was hired to write some additional tunes, along with Harry B. Smith. This is one of them. It is also a love song.

(To really get the feeling and the impact of this comparison, it is necessary to find recordings of these two songs, both readily available. I checked them out from the New York Public Library.)

My desert is waiting, dear.
Come there with me.
I'm longing to teach you
Love's sweet melody.
I'll sing a love song to you,
Painting a picture for two.

Blue heaven and you and I
And sand kissing a moonlit sky.
The desert breeze whisp'ring a lullaby,
Only stars above you
To see I love you.

Oh, give me that night divine,
And let my arms in yours entwine.

The desert song calling,
Its voice enthralling
Will make you mine!

The lyrics were "operetta-poetic."

That, of course, is "The Desert Song." Now, "They Didn't Believe Me."

And when I told them
How beautiful you are,
They didn't believe me.
They didn't believe me.

Your lips, your eyes,
Your cheeks, your hair,
Are in a class beyond compare.
You're the loveliest girl
That one could see.

And when I tell them,
And I'm certainly going to tell them,
That I'm the man whose wife

One day you'll be,
They'll never believe me.
They'll never believe me
That from this great big world
You've chosen me.

The first number, "The Desert Song," is a waltz. "They Didn't Believe Me" is in 4/4 time and thirty-two bars (which was to become the standard for the American popular ballad). Both songs have very strong melodies. It is my guess that both were written music first. And while I haven't the musical skill or vocabulary to explain the difference between the songs musically, all you have to do is listen to them side by side and it becomes clear that there is an enormous difference between the two songs. "The Desert Song" sounds dated. Not only are the lyrics "operetta-poetic," but the melody itself seems indistinguishable from the European melodies on which it is modeled. "They'd Never Believe Me," on the other hand, sounds fresh and new and "available." And "American." Not only is the lyric easy and natural, sounding the way someone would actually speak, but the melody is "easy" too, catchy and hummable and devoid of pretension.

Jerome Kern was born, neither in middle Europe nor in a vaudeville trunk, but in a middle-class New York home. His mother was a pianist and a piano teacher. His father owned a department store. Jerome studied at the New York College of Music for a year or so, and then he persuaded his reluctant parents to send him to Europe for a year where, in London, he managed to get a few unimportant songwriting assignments for minor British musicals.

How different it was then. It is hard for us to imagine. Here is a kid, eighteen or nineteen years old, who travels to London and, with no significant connections, gets odd jobs writing songs for West End shows. How could such a thing happen? It reminds me of my great drama teacher, B. Iden Payne, talking about his youthful days in the theatre in England when, as a boy of fifteen or sixteen, he quit school and joined a Shakespearean touring company because, as he said, "You could always get a job in the theatre."

This is a different world we are talking about. A world without radio. A world without television. A world without film. If you wanted to be entertained (and everyone wants to be entertained) you had to leave your home and go someplace, to a theater or a concert hall, where real, live people were there to entertain you.

There were hundreds of shows in those days. Hundreds. And that was just in New York. If you counted the circuits and the wheels and the legitimate theatres and the opera houses around the country (any country), there were thousands of shows, all of them employing actors and singers and musicians. In the last years of the 20's, even with the competition of movies (silent movies), there were regularly about four hundred plays done each year on Broadway, and fifty or sixty new musicals. In the last few years there have not been enough new musicals to find four to nominate for Tony Awards.

At the time when Jerome Kern was starting out, not only were there a lot of shows produced each year, in New York and London and elsewhere, but new musicals made it a practice to incorporate songs from more than one composer. That is how young Jerome picked up a few bucks (or quid, as the case may be) by grinding out a few tunes for British shows.

When he returned to New York in 1904, he had definitely decided to try his luck in the field of musical theatre, and he went about it in an extraordinarily sane and practical way. First he got a job at Harms Music as a song-plugger. His champion there was none other than Max Dreyfus, whom you will remember from the room with the Barca Loungers. Since Harms was primarily the publisher for show music, Kern became friendly with people in the business, and it wasn't long before he had moved up from song-plugger to rehearsal pianist.

He was young. He was friendly. And he was ambitious. Whenever there was a break in the rehearsal for lunch or for a "take five," he would stay at the piano and play some of his own tunes "just for fun." The chorus kids gathered around and, eventually, the director, choreographer, and even the producer or producers. It didn't take long for everyone to realize that these tunes were better than the ones in the show. (I will assume that the other composers did not gather around the piano to "ooh" and "ah." I will further assume that the other composer or composers were probably not even considered important enough to be at the rehearsals.)

The Princess Theater, home for a new kind of musical in a 299-seat house.

Anyway, some of these songs began to be incorporated into some of these shows, one thing led to another, and between 1905 and 1910, Kern had songs in twenty-one different musicals. In 1915, Kern began his long association with English-born librettist Guy Bolton. There was a little theater in New York (and I do mean little, 299 seats) called the Princess Theater. The producer was having trouble finding anything to fit there, and he finally decided (surprisingly) to try the idea of small musicals. In other words, a novelty. And thus it was that Kern and Bolton were hired to write a small musical, and the Princess Theater shows were born, a milestone in the history of the American musical theatre.

It was a daring idea.

There wasn't room (or money) for elaborate scenery, so they decided there would be two sets, one for each act. The orchestra would be limited to eleven pieces. And the cast would be small.

Of course, "small" is a relative term. "Small" at the Princess Theater meant thirty people. (And this in a 299 seat house!) Thus have the economics changed. *Our Town* is now considered unworkable for a regular run with a cast of twenty-four. When it opened originally in 1938 it had a cast of forty-seven. Actors were cheaper in 1938. And they were a lot cheaper in 1915. (Not to mention musicians and stagehands!)

Still, there is no question that the Princess Theater shows were small by the standards of their time. And it was a very daring thing to attempt.

In addition to size, there were other experiments that Kern wished to undertake. He had had enough of shows with a grab-bag of songs by many composers. He had also had more than his share of working over stale, imported operettas. He was determined to help create a new kind of show with a contemporary story and contemporary characters, a show where the songs were not merely a collection of good tunes with catchy titles but actually came out of the people and the situations.

Theory, of course, is one thing, and practice is another. A new concept, however brilliant, does not come easily. All of which is to say that the first of the Princess Theater shows, called *Nobody's Perfect*, didn't manage to accomplish many of the new ideas except for the reduced size. The second attempt, *Very Good Eddie*, had a contemporary setting and story, and it made a modest attempt to extract the humor from the characters and the situation instead of from some vaudeville routines. The songs had that special Kern style, and there were no interpolations. Fortunately it was a huge hit, and the Princess Theater shows were on their way.

Only two sets per show, but actors were still cheap (and plentiful). (From *Very Good Eddie*)

Shortly after *Eddie* opened, Bolton introduced Kern to an old British chum of his, P. G. Wodehouse, and the three of them teamed up on a series of shows with Kern doing the music, Wodehouse the lyrics, and Bolton and Wodehouse collaborating on the book. Two of these shows, *Oh, Boy* and *Leave it to Jane*, became big hits, but by the 1920's the Princess Theater shows had had their day, and the three collaborators moved on to successful careers in the regular Broadway theatre.

Following in their wake were a whole series of musicals, more or less directly influenced by the Princess Theater shows. Among the writers were DeSylva, Henderson and Brown (*Good News*), Vincent Youmans (*No, No, Nanette*), and Dietz and Schwartz (*The Bandwagon*), as well as such pantheon composers and lyricists as Yip Harburg, Harold Arlen, Burton Lane, and Dorothy Fields. And in categories all by themselves: the Gershwins, Rodgers and Hart, Cole Porter, and Irving Berlin.

Nearly all the shows by these writers were set in contemporary America. Their music was popular music, usually following the aaba form. The lyrics were slangy and urban. There was no feeling of operetta about them at all. And yet the transition dreamed of by Jerome Kern had not yet been fully made. For one thing, the songs, though fitting into the general pattern and "feeling" of the shows, did not truly come out of character or situation, except in the most general sense. Songs cut from one show were reinserted into another. It made no difference. The songwriters were what mattered, the style of the songwriters. People wanted to hear a Gershwin song, or a Cole Porter song, or an Irving Berlin song. They didn't want the style sublimated to characters or story. They wanted to savor the lyrics and the melodies for their wit and slang and style rather than for their dramatic verity.

It remained for Jerome Kern, working with Oscar Hammerstein in 1927, to open the door to the new way with *Showboat*. And it remained for Oscar Hammerstein, working in 1943 with Richard Rodgers (Kern had just died), to take the next logical step with *Oklahoma!*

4

Rodgers and Hammerstein

There has been a great deal written about this fabled collaboration. After being considered somewhat "out of fashion" for a while, they have been critically rediscovered and re-evaluated. Beginning with the 50th anniversary of *Oklahoma!* and followed by acclaimed productions of *Carousel* and *The King and I*, Rodgers and Hammerstein have been the subject of a steady stream of books and articles as well as the source of constant albums and revivals. (Even *State Fair*, the movie for which they wrote eight songs in 1945, was resurrected for Broadway in 1996.)

In view of this vast deluge, it is possible that you have had your fill of R & H history, in which case you may be tempted to skip ahead to more recent writers. The fact remains, however, that this collaboration was the crucial melding that brought together operetta and the Broadway showbiz tradition born out of "variety." This was, and to a large extent, *is* what we are talking about when we speak of the American musical.

Therefore, I will try to be brief (difficult to do with two such extraordinary careers) and try to focus on exactly what it was that they accomplished and how it changed the shape and form of American theatre.

Before *Oklahoma!*, they had each done twenty-five Broadway musicals, Hammerstein with a variety of composers, Rodgers with only one lyricist. Although they had not worked together, their lives had been curiously intertwined. Both went to Columbia University. Rodgers was seven years younger than Hammerstein, but his older brother, Mortimer, was in the same class as Oscar and performed with him in varsity shows. Later, when Rodgers was old enough to enter college, ex-student Hammerstein was on the board that selected Rodgers' show for the varsity. They even wrote one song together at that time.

However, it is instructive to look at their early careers separately to see what each of them was to bring to this fabled partnership. And since Oscar was the elder and began his career first, we will start with him.

Oscar Hammerstein II

As we have seen before, Oscar Hammerstein came from a theatrical family. His grandfather, Oscar the first, produced operas and operettas, among them *Naughty Marietta*. His father, William Hammerstein, managed the Victoria Theater, which his grandfather owned. His uncle, Arthur Hammerstein, produced musicals, including those by both Friml and Romberg.

Oscar's family wanted him to go into law, but after a taste of the varsity shows at Columbia, he decided to give up school and get a job working around the family's theatrical empire. He stage-managed or assisted on several of his uncle's musicals, and eventually tried his hand at writing. His first professional work, a straight play produced by Uncle Arthur, closed in New Haven after scathing notices and no business. His second attempt (how lucky to have a second attempt!) was an assignment doing both book and lyrics for another of his uncle's shows. Arthur, deciding that Oscar's talent was stronger for lyrics than book, teamed him up with Otto Harbach, who took the young man under his wing and began to teach him the craft of putting together a musical, at least, as musicals existed at that time.

For several years, Oscar wrote lyrics and sometimes collaborated on the libretto for a number of musicals, usually with Otto Harbach. In the beginning, the music was by Herbert Stothart, but later Oscar worked with such well-known composers as Vincent Youmans, Rudolph Friml, Jerome Kern, and, on one occasion only, George Gershwin. That show was called *Song of the Flame*, and its abrupt failure helped convince Hammerstein to stick to the world of operetta rather than the world of Broadway show-biz. For it was in operetta that he felt he could help create a new American folk musical with some of the integration that existed in opera.

It is important to note, by the way, that during this entire time, with all these many partners, the customary work method for Hammerstein was to set lyrics to music already composed. He said later, in his excellent book, *Lyrics*, that this was because so many of his early collaborators were middle European in origin and their unfamiliarity with the rhythms of the English language would have made it difficult for them to work the other way around—lyrics first. While there is undoubtedly some truth in this, it is also true that this was the standard way of writing songs for most collaborators in those days. Perhaps this was so because the first big hits were imported from Europe, and English lyrics had to be put to previously established music. Perhaps it was because of the language problem that

Hammerstein suggests. But I think it is more likely that it happened because this is not an illogical way to work. Find the melodies that set the emotional mood and then set appropriate lyrics to match. Rodgers and Hart worked that way. So did George and Ira Gershwin. So, frequently, did Lerner and Loewe. So, in the beginning, did Stephen Sondheim when he set lyrics to *West Side Story* and *Gypsy*.

Hammerstein before Rodgers: *Showboat*, 1927. An experiment that wasn't repeated until 1943.

In 1927, Jerome Kern obtained the rights to Edna Ferber's novel *Showboat* and asked Oscar Hammerstein to do the book and lyrics. (It was, by the way, the first time that Hammerstein had done the book completely on his own from the start.) Oscar jumped at the chance. Here it was, the opportunity to do an adult American musical with a composer who had pioneered the ideas of musical integration and songs coming out of character. The two writers worked in perfect harmony, and when they were finished, they took the show to Florenz Ziegfeld (of all people) with whom they had had a hit some years back with *Sunny*, starring Marilyn Miller. Surprisingly, Ziegfeld agreed to produce *Showboat* in his theatre after the current hit *Rio Rita* closed.

According to his secretary, whom I saw interviewed in the fascinating television teaching series, *Broadway, A Musical History*, put together by Ron Housman, Ziegfeld hated the whole thing. The girls wore too many clothes. There wasn't enough comedy. It was too serious. But these were two hot writers and they had given him a hit, so he went along with it. His secretary, Goldie (remembered fondly by Moss Hart in *Act One*), recalled that Mr. Ziegfeld particularly hated "Ol' Man River" and tried his damnedest to get it taken out of the show. On opening night, there was little applause during the show. The audience was stunned. They had never seen anything like it, and especially not here, at the Ziegfeld Theater. "Ziggy" sat on the steps to the balcony, alternately weeping and fuming. "I knew it!" he kept muttering: "I knew I shouldn't have produced this goddamned show!"

Of course, the next day when the press was ecstatic and there were lines two blocks long outside the theatre, all was forgiven and, presumably, forgotten. No producer, nor indeed anyone else, remembers their doubts after a show has become an established hit. In hindsight we are all geniuses.

What are the things that distinguish *Showboat*, that make it different? The serious plot, for one thing. There is not even a happy ending in the usual musical comedy sense. The songs came out of the characters in a way not done before. There was the panoramic picture of American over three decades; as the country changes, the characters change, too. Last but certainly not least, there was a sympathetic story involving miscegenation, a subject unbelievably daring at the time.

Let me intrude here for a moment to explain, to those who are too young to remember, the way it used to be. In 1954, when I first arrived in New York and had the first showing of my work in a revue, the outstanding number from that production was booked, and then cancelled, by the *Ed Sullivan Show* because it showed white children and black children playing together. Not kissing, not hugging, not making it in the back of a convertible. Just playing kid's games together out in the street. CBS was afraid that their Southern affiliates might be upset. Not long after that, Harry Belafonte, touring a concert show with Marge and Gower Champion, had to be concealed and sneaked into hotels all across the South and West because "coloreds" were not allowed. And this at a time when Belafonte was already a recording star with careers both in television and film! Remember, we are talking about the 1950's. Imagine what it must have been like in 1928!

Looking across the perspective of time, the most striking thing about *Showboat* is that it did not start a trend, even with the two men who had created it. Despite its enormous success, there were no shows following in its path. Hammerstein's next musical, *New Moon*, was in the tried and true operetta tradition. After that, he had eight "musical comedies" in a row which opened on Broadway and promptly failed. Many people thought his career was over.

They were wrong.

Richard Rodgers

Richard Rodgers learned to play the piano at a very early age. He wrote his first song (for a camp show) at fourteen. He had acquired a partner by the age of sixteen. And he had his first song in a Broadway musical at the ripe old age of seventeen. (That song, by the way, called *Any Old Place with You*, contained the memorable rhyme: "I'd go to hell for yuh, even Philadelphia!" and stands up very well today.)

The partner, of course, was Lorenz Hart, who was also seven years older than Rodgers, and who felt that lyric writing could be more than just fitting round vowels to fruity music, which was the case with many of the operettas so popular at the time.

After that brief Broadway introduction, Rodgers entered Columbia University, primarily for the opportunity to work on the annual varsity show. He immediately wrote a show which was accepted (the only freshman ever to do so) and this production, with lyrics by Hart, who was a Columbia graduate, was covered by the New York critics. After it received good notices, Broadway producers came, too. One of them, Lew Fields, decided to take a chance and let the young team do the complete score for his next show, *Poor Little Ritz Girl*. They wrote twelve songs, which Fields bought. But partly because they were young and inexperienced and partly because he felt the show needed the "security," eight of the songs were thrown out in Boston and replaced with a new score written by Sigmund Romberg.

By the way, Rodgers and Hart were a "team." Up to that time, one spoke of a Victor Herbert show, or a Sigmund Romberg show, or a Friml or a Kern show. Now, for the first time, the lyricist was given equal recognition along with the composer. And who knows? If Richard Rodgers had been seven years older than Lorenz Hart, rather than the other way around, it might have turned out differently.

After that big disappointment in Boston with *Poor Little Ritz Girl*, in 1920, Rodgers and Hart continued to do songs whenever and wherever they could, until five years later when they finally got their second chance. It happened almost by accident. The Theatre Guild had just built their new theater, but they had run short of cash before they were able to purchase new drapes. So it was decided that the Guild would sponsor a small revue to show off the talents of some of the younger members of the organization and to raise money for the desired drapes.

There were to be two performances, matinee and evening, May 17, 1925, at the Garrick Theater, and the revue was to be called *The Garrick Gaieties*. It had a cast of unknown performers, many of whom were to go on to fame and fortune. Lee Strasberg was in it. So was Sandy Meisner. The stage managers were Harold Clurman and Cheryl Crawford. In short, if a bomb had been dropped on the theatre, not only would there have been no Rodgers and Hart, there would also have been no Group Theatre, no Actors Studio, and no "Method." (And all that that implies.)

The two performances were extended to six, and then to six months. There was also a *Gaieties* the following year. And in between the two, Rodgers and Hart wrote *Dearest Enemy* and *The Girl Friend* with their friend and collaborator Herbert Fields. Though these two musicals didn't create much of a stir, their next project, *A Connecticut Yankee in King Arthur's Court*, turned out to be a great hit with a score rich with standards such as "Thou Swell" and "My Heart Stood Still."

Throughout the next decade, the team alternated between standard Broadway-type musical comedies and wild, far-out experiments. *Peggy Ann* was a Freudian dream with a prologue and an epilogue. There was no opening chorus of singers (as in *Oklahoma!* many years later). There was no song at all for the first fifteen minutes. The epilogue was played in almost total darkness. *Chee-Chee* tried to use songs of many different styles and lengths, some of them only a few lines long. There was no listing of musical numbers in the program.

In 1936, for the first time, they did a show that was to have a real influence on the form of the musical. It was *On Your Toes*, for which they wrote the book along with George Abbott. They decided to incorporate dance as an integral part of the story and hired a classical choreographer, George Balanchine, to stage the dances, the most memorable of which was "Slaughter on Tenth Avenue," a full-length jazz ballet.

Rodgers before Hammerstein: "Slaughter on Tenth Avenue," a full-length jazz ballet featured in *On Your Toes*. Pictured above, with his back to the camera, alongside Tamara Geva and Ray Bolger, is George Church, who later danced Jud in the "Dream Ballet" in *Oklahoma!* Incidentally, Rodgers used a dream ballet to close the first act of *Pal Joey* a few years before Agnes De Mille and *Oklahoma!*

The show was so successful that the producer, Dwight Deere Wiman, commissioned two more with choreography by Balanchine. In 1937 it was *Babes in Arms*. In 1938 it was *I Married an Angel*. In 1940 they wrote what was to be the pinnacle of their collaboration, *Pal Joey*, with a libretto by John O'Hara, based on his *New Yorker* stories. What was so special about it? Well, of course, the score, but even more so, the book, the flavor, the very idea. Joey is a heel. And he is a hero. Or perhaps we should say he is an anti-hero, the first one in the musical theatre.

After their next show, *By Jupiter*, the partnership began to slowly dissolve. Of course, most partnerships do in time, but this partnership in particular was troubled by more than the usual disenchantment of too much extended proximity. Lorenz Hart, who was abnormally small, almost a midget, was a troubled man. He was an alcoholic. He was given to fits of deep depression. He was increasingly unpredictable and unprofessional. His younger partner was just the opposite: controlled, (some said) cold, and the absolute professional. In time things became so bad that Rodgers had to lock Hart in his hotel room to get him to finish a lyric. It couldn't last, and it didn't. In 1941, Rodgers had secretly become co-producer, along with George Abbott, of the hit *Best Foot Forward*. He had also spoken to Oscar Hammerstein about the possibility of their working together should the partnership with Hart ever break up.

When Theresa Helburn of the Theatre Guild approached Rodgers about making a musical of an old Guild play, *Green Grow the Lilacs* by Lynn Riggs, Rodgers was interested. Hart was not. (It wasn't, after all, his cup of tea.) And thus it was that Rodgers made that call to Hammerstein. Hammerstein was more than interested. He was ecstatic. He himself had tried several times to persuade Jerome Kern to work on this very same play, and he knew in his bones that it was just right for his particular sensibilities and talents.

Oklahoma!

What is it that is so special about *Oklahoma!*? We know that it ran a long time, over five years. We know it continues to be performed around the country and around the world. We know that it became a successful movie and contained lots of hit songs. We know that it established the team of Rodgers and Hammerstein, and we know that they went on to write many other successful and influential musicals.

We also know that it affected the form of the American musical. But how? From what to what? In what way was *Oklahoma!* different from what had gone before? To best answer that question, let's compare it to the primary sources, or types, which had preceded it.

First, let's compare it to operetta. What are the similarities and what are the differences? Well, like much of American operetta, it is set in the past. It has an exotic locale: Oklahoma Indian Territory at the turn of the century. Its use of the singing chorus is similar to operetta: i.e. the arrival of neighboring cowhands and farmers' daughters at the appropriate moments to augment the singing and dancing. And, while this might be said to be true of all musical comedy at that time, *Oklahoma!* is imbued with a folksy optimism that seems to suggest operetta much more than it does the typical Broadway musical of the early 40's.

What are the differences between *Oklahoma!* and the typical operetta? For one thing, the "tone" is different. The music and lyrics are simpler and more direct than those in operetta. The show has an American, not a European, sound. (Compare it, for example, to *Naughty Marietta*, also set in early Americana.) There are no spectacular scenic effects. Dance is an important part of the story. Plot is less elaborate than in operetta. Character is more important than plot; for here, as in all good drama, character and plot are hard to separate.

Now let's compare *Oklahoma!* to the "showbiz" shows by the Gershwins, Rodgers and Hart, Cole Porter, Irving Berlin, and the other major musical writers of the 30's and early 40's. What are the similarities and what are the differences? In my opinion, the score is the most striking similarity. As we noted, the score wasn't European in feeling, it was very much American, very much in the simple, straightforward, classic Broadway show song style. The things that made the show different were the things that made it more like operetta (see above). It was "period." It wasn't "contemporary." It didn't have that slangy, "now" feeling of the 30's shows. And it was more romantic in an old-fashioned way.

Oklahoma! became, in effect, the wedding of operetta and "variety," a put-together by two masters who were at the peak of their form. *Show Boat* had paved the way, but despite the fact that it was very successful, it was still ahead of its time. And whereas *Show Boat* spawned no immediate imitators, *Oklahoma!* quickly became the role model for most of the American musicals of the next decade—and beyond.

Readiness, as Shakespeare shrewdly observed, is all. And the time was right for *Oklahoma!*. Consider this point: Hammerstein's last big hits had been *Show Boat* and *New Moon*, both done in 1928. After that he had eight flops in a row on Broadway, until he did *Oklahoma!* in 1943. What happened? Did he lose his talent? Did he have bad luck? Or was it something different, something more basic than that? Well, I must confess that I don't really know those unsuccessful shows, but I do have a theory about what happened.

Those last big hits were in 1928. A significant date:

the time of the stockmarket crash that signaled the onslaught of the Great Depression. And the Depression was not a time of serene optimism, nor was it a time for celebrating the golden memory of America's idealized past. It was a slangy time, a skeptical time, and the optimism was of a particular kind. American history was not Oklahoma Indian Territory; it was the little guys against the bosses. It was Gary Cooper against Edward Arnold. It was the new against the old, and the new was in the right (meaning, in this case, the Left). "They call us babes in arms, but we are babes in armor!"

In short, it was not Oscar Hammerstein's time. 1934 was not his time; 1943 was. 1943! The country was united. The tide of the war was beginning to turn. The enemy was Evil with a capital E. We were clearly the good guys. It was a time for moral certainty, for hope, for dreams, for celebration of a warm, wonderful America that used to be.

When Mike Todd saw *Oklahoma!* (then known as *Away We Go*) out of town, he shook his head and said succinctly: "No girls. No gags. No chance." A couple of years earlier he might have been right. Now he was wrong. The great wheel turns. This time it turned in favor of Oscar Hammerstein. And Mike Todd and his brand of snappy Broadway-type showbiz was suddenly an endangered species, soon to be replaced by an infinite number of little *Oklahoma!*s, some of them lousy, and an amazing number of them good, even wonderful.

5

THE BREAKUP OF THE FORM

If you look at some of the musicals in the years just before *Oklahoma!*, and then look at some of the musicals in the years just after *Oklohama!*, you will see that there was a profound change in the form of the musical, one which enabled these later works to survive and become part of the ongoing dramatic literature of our time, whereas the earlier ones are now nearly forgotten relics.

Oklahoma! opened in 1943. For the next three decades, the American musical continued to be based primarily on this Rodgers and Hammerstein form. For example, it is clear that Alan Jay Lerner and Frederick L. Loewe followed Rodgers and Hammerstein when they did *Brigadoon* They emulated them not only in the primacy of the book and integration of the elements, but in many of the specifics, as well. The setting was far away and exotic. Though Tommy and Jeff are modern, most of the characters are from eighteenth-century Scotland. Indeed, the very point of the piece is that the values and style of the earlier period are better than those of today.

The secondary lovers in *Brigadoon* owe a lot to Ado Annie and Will Parker, just as the dark villain, thwarted in love, owes much to Jud. And, as with *Oklahoma!*, Agnes de Mille was there to supply plot-oriented ballets.

There is in Lerner and Loewe's work, as there was in most of the Rodgers and Hammerstein shows, a clear connection to the world of operetta. (Fritz Loewe was a direct descendant of the Viennese operetta.) Look at the settings: *Paint Your Wagon* took place in California during the Gold Rush days. *My Fair Lady* was set in Edwardian England. The next (a film) was *Gigi*: fin de siècle Paris. *Camelot* was set in King Arthur's court. And finally *On a Clear Day*, which Lerner did with Burton Lane, was about a split personality living, or reliving, part of her previous incarnation in Georgian England.

But the basic point is that the R & H form was dominant, not only in Lerner and Loew, who clearly were kindred spirits. It was also dominant in *Gypsy*, which came, not from the operetta tradition, but from the Broadway, or "variety" tradition. It was dominant in *Fiddler on the Roof*, which was from a different milieu altogether. Indeed, it was dominant in almost everything, from *The Music Man* and *Hello, Dolly!* and *She Loves Me* and *Carnival* to *Sweet Charity* and *Promises, Promises* and *Cabaret*.

Everyone knew and understood the rules. To do a Broadway musical, this is what you did:

You "acquired a property," a story with some color and splash and sympathetic characters. It could be Thornton Wilder's *The Matchmaker* or Shaw's *Pygmalion* or even Eugene O'Neill's *Ah, Wilderness!*. Possibly it might be a movie, like *The Apartment* or *Lili* or *The Little Shop Around The Corner*. Sometimes you did an original, but not often.

You laid out the proposed "property" in musical form. You "blocked it out" and indicated places for songs and dances.

You cut the play script down to the bone.

You found a place to insert a chorus of singers and dancers.

You wrote songs.

You took it to Boston (or Philadelphia or someplace).

You rewrote and restaged (and sometimes recast) on the road.

You brought it into New York City.

You had a real Opening Night. All the critics were there at the same time, plus all the luminaries and the opinion-makers.

You either had a big hit or a big flop, or sometimes (though not often) you might have something in-between.

And throughout, you were guided by certain clear principles about which everybody—writers, directors, producers, actors, audiences, and even critics—agreed. Namely:

1. The musical had to fulfill the needs of the story and the characters. The book was primary and basic.
2. All the elements had to be integrated into a unified whole, a cohesive work of art.
3. There had to be a sense of movement, of change, of many scenes and lots of scenery. (Though the scenery did not necessarily have to be spectacular; the key was change more than spectacle.)
4. There had to be lots of singing and dancing, and lots of people to sing and dance.
5. By and large, the songs had to be strongly melodic, and simple enough to "grasp" on first hearing. And usually there were enough reprises to guarantee that you could whistle at least one tune as you walked out of the theatre.
6. The basic message of the show had to be positive. Bad things could happen, but it had to turn out all right.

7. The characters could, and should, be interesting, but they couldn't be too "complex." There wasn't time.
8. Lastly, no matter how serious the show might get, no matter how elevated the theme—there had to be *entertainment*. There had to be variety, both in scenes and in songs, and you'd better, by God, have some humor. If Shakespeare could manage laughs, plenty of them, in *Hamlet*, you could do it with your little musical comedy.

These eight basic principles were the guide for the Broadway musical. They were unquestioned. They were the heart of what we call the R & H style. They were second nature to those who wrote for the musical theatre. And they are still viable today. But—they are no longer *the guide*.

Something happened.

Somehow they lost favor, if not with the audiences at large, at least with many of the most influential theatre people on Broadway. To begin with, they lost favor with the most powerful of the critics.

What happened? Why should these precepts, which had guided the most popular and distinguished of our musicals, suddenly be questioned? There were several reasons. Among them:

Time. Things change. The wheel turns. Nothing stays the same. Iambic pentameter and open verse, surely the most flexible tools in the history of the English speaking stage, went out of fashion, to be followed by elaborate prose, to be followed by terse prose, to be followed by—what? A lyric theatre, perhaps. Who knows; maybe even by iambic pentameter again.

Predictability. The form of these musicals became predictable. Perhaps they had been *too* successful. The form was too well known. Too many people had studied it. You could tell, after a while, how it was going to "breathe" in and out. You could anticipate the production number, the use of the chorus, the lead-in to the next song. You knew that there would be a certain kind of number for the leading character at a certain place. Some people liked knowing this. It reassured them. Others didn't like it. Young people in particular, both writers and critics, wanted change. The tone of the times changed. The rather smug optimism of World War II and its aftermath was replaced gradually by a growing realization of the complexity of things. America became, for better or worse, a part of the complex global geopolitical game. Old certainties were no longer so certain. We did not always "win," we found out. Good guys were sometimes bad guys and vice versa. The heady optimism which informed most of these musicals began to be questioned. The economics changed. The out of town tryout became prohibitively expensive. The financing of a Broadway musical became harder and harder. (This calls to mind a story about Mel Brooks when he was the book-writer for *All American* in the early 60's. When he was told that the show broke even at eighty thousand dollars a week, he replied: "Eighty thousand! Brazil breaks even at eighty thousand a week!" Of course, now the figure would be more like three hundred thousand, or more. The recent revival of *Showboat* reportedly broke even at six hundred thousand!) Because of the economics, fewer and fewer shows were being done, and more and more of those were tried out in England first, where the costs were not so high and where at times the productions were partly underwritten by the subsidized theatres.

Rising out of the somnolence of the 50's, and affected by the permissiveness of education, young people rebelled against the values of their parents, and a major part of this rebellion was spearheaded in the field of music. Beginning in the 60's, and continuing up to the present time, pop music and show music split. For the first time in this century, the American musical ceased to be a source of popular music.

In light of these various converging factors, people began to question the R & H model, and people began to search for something else to take its place. Among the experiments tried so far are:

Dance Musicals and the Ascent of the Choreographer

This was not really a specific attack on the form, but rather a re-interpretation of it. As we have noted, the primacy of the book is the single most important tenet of the R & H form. The second most important "rule" is the integration of all the diverse aspects into one unified whole. Increasingly, the role of central "unifier" fell to the director-choreographer.

West Side Story, 1957—the ascent of the director-choreographer.

Beginning with Jerome Robbins and *West Side Story* and going on through Gower Champion and Bob Fosse and

Michael Bennett and Tommy Tune, the director-choreographer frequently became the center not only of the production but of the script and score as well. Some of their shows had books (most of them, in fact) but it was the director-choreographer who had the power. He would say: "We need another song here, a production number." Or: "No, that solo is no good. Make it a duet for two secondary characters." Just as he might say: "This scene doesn't work. We need a comic beat here, not an introspection" or whatever. Sometimes it was all for the best. Sometimes not. One thing is clear, however. Director-choreographers are not, by training or inclination, "book-people." The primacy of the book began to erode—to the point where, in *A Chorus Line* or *Nine* or *Will Rogers Follies*, the writers were just hired to "fill in" the director's vision. The "shaping" became everything. The form, the book, the score, the characters—they were all just part of the composite picture, no more important, ultimately, than the lights or the sound or the sets. The "put together" was king.

"Concept Musicals"

What were they? What are they?

Ultimately, they are musicals in which the style is considered as important as the content, where the style rather than the book may be the unifying element.

As far as I know, the idea came from Harold Prince, working principally on musicals by Stephen Sondheim. I'm not sure when the concept was first articulated, but I seem to remember that it was very much influenced by Prince's work with the stage designer Boris Aronson who, in *Company* and then in many other Prince-Sondheim shows, conceived a central scenic metaphor which helped cohere and inform the whole piece.

Harold Prince received his training at the hands of George Abbott, an early version of the "put-together" artist, for Abbott not only produced and directed his shows, he also co-authored them. As I understand it, he didn't create the characters or the plot or even the dialogue (though he had proven himself capable as a writer in all those categories). His job was to supervise the "put-together." What follows what—and for how long—and how often? What do you cut? What do you add? How do you shape it? How do fix it when it's wrong?

After Abbott, who was the master of the musical form of the 40's and 50's, Prince worked with (and was influenced by) Jerome Robbins, who was also a protégé of Abbott's and the unquestioned master of the musical form during the 50's and 60's. Under these two men, and after a long learning process, Prince became himself an expert at the "put-together." Gradually, after years of producing, he moved up to become what he had always wanted to be—a director and a master of the form for the 70's and 80's (and possibly the 90's as well).

The "concept" musical was not a new idea. It was an extension of the cohesion process begun under R & H, except in this case the idea was carried even further. What it meant was that, unlike Rodgers and Hammerstein or Lerner and Loewe, who simply found a good story and musicalized it, now it was considered appropriate (and artistically more satisfying) to have a vision of the whole show, a style/metaphor "concept" which would not only guide the director and the designer but the writer and composer as well. Thus, in *Follies* the "concept" was the interplay of two sets of characters, the older disillusioned Follies girls of "Now" with their younger, idealistic selves of "Then." In *Pacific Overtures*, the concept was to mix the styles of Japanese kabuki with the music hall and vaudeville routines of the West. *In Sweeney Todd* the concept was to hang the whole stage with elements of a period factory, playing out one man's cruelty against the backdrop of the industrial cruelty that produced it.

The Concept Musical. An early Boris Aronson sketch for *Follies*, 1971.

Later, Michael Bennett, who had done choreography for some of these concept musicals, had an idea, a concept, of his own: a chorus line—a line upon the stage which Broadway dancers, auditioning for the chorus line in a new show, would either step across and be accepted or stay behind and be dismissed.

Rock Musicals

In the 1960's there was a cultural upheaval in this country. Prompted by the Vietnam War and presaged by the young people's increasing rebelliousness in the late 1950's, there was a sudden and severe clash between the old and the new.

Clothing, which had been relatively sedate since the last "upheaval" of the 1920's, suddenly became aggressively loud and "different." The neat, trimmed hair styles of the first half of the twentieth century became long and stringy and wild, for both men and women. The "pill" suddenly made sex seem less perilous than before, and in contrast to the prudishness which had prevailed in this country since its Puritan origins, all at once everything seemed possible—and permissible. Pornography became readily available. Homosexuals declared themselves openly and proudly, and many began to organize as a political force. Sex at all levels and in all forms was suddenly the order of the day. As one song lyric put it at the time: "Come join the holy Kama-Sutra orgy everyone!"

Drugs entered the culture in a big way, starting with marijuana and LSD and escalating in some cases into "uppers" and "downers," "speed," "horse," and, of course, "coke." The times, they were a-changing. The flower children tuned in and dropped out. African Americans began to acquire, a hundred years late, their promised civil rights. There were distant stirrings among the women of the land, talk of "feminism" and "chauvinist pigs." The Viet Cong and the young men of America killed each other in bloody combat every evening on the national news. The young men in the National Guard killed the kids on the campus. And out of the turmoil and confusion, Richard Nixon, like the phoenix, rose again out of the ashes of his own political immolation.

Throughout most of the period, Broadway continued on its old way. The biggest hit of the decade was *Hello, Dolly!* The second biggest was *Fiddler on the Roof*. Then, as the 60's were drawing to a close, the cultural upheaval finally hit the theatre. *Hair* opened, and ran and ran and ran, and toured and toured and toured. It boasted a rock score, one of the first to hit Broadway (although *Bye Bye Birdie* had introduced some Presley-like moments as early as 1960). It spoke out openly against the war and for the sexual revolution. It made no secret of its drug connections; quite the contrary, that was part of its appeal. It displayed full frontal nudity of both men and women for the first time on the Broadway stage, and that was part of its appeal, as well.

Hair, 1968—the presentation of a lifestyle, an "event."

In addition, there was one other significant development: namely, *Hair* had no "book" in the normal sense of the word. When it first opened, at Joseph Papp's Public Theatre, under the direction of Gerald Freedman, it did have a book, a book about a young boy called up for service in the Vietnam War. Later, when the show was moved, first to a disco called Cheetah, and then to the Barrymore Theatre on Broadway, the authors, rebellious not only towards the national culture but also to the traditions of the stage, got rid of Gerald Freedman and hired instead Tom O'Horgan, who had established himself as one of the foremost directors of the new avant-garde.

Together, the director and the writers (who were also the leading players) threw out the linear plot and introduced instead something new. It was more like a revue than a regular book musical. But really, it was something else: the presentation of a lifestyle, an alternative to the usual Broadway score, and an alternative to the normal Broadway moral values (which were still connected to the optimism of the old Rodgers and Hammerstein days).

People loved it. (At least, a great many people did; there were those, in the theatre and elsewhere, who deplored its self-indulgence.) The score, in my opinion, was a very good one, with lots of new and surprising verbal images and consistently tuneful and exciting music. The frontal nudity was of interest to everyone, no matter what they may have said. And most of all, *Hair* was an experience, an "event." It was something to talk about, both pro and con. It was a "must," for the cognoscenti as well as for every teenager and college student in America. And it made money as if it were a printing machine at Fort Knox.

But was it a trend? That was the hot question at the time. Was this the wave of the future? Clive Barnes, then the all-powerful critic for the *New York Times*, thought so. He lauded the show over and over again. He socialized with its creators. He wrote that the days of the old linear (book) musical were dead. Or, as one might paraphrase it: "I have seen the future, and it is anarchy." For, ultimately, that was what the show was. There was no structure, no discipline, only the exhilaration of the moment, perhaps boosted by a few drugs. And, looking at the history of any art, it becomes clear that structure and discipline are necessary for any form which is to take hold and become the basis for new development.

This is not to say that rock music has no place in the musical theatre. Quite the contrary. It is one of the major influences now at work, as the recent success of *Tommy* and, especially, *Rent* attests.

There is an enormous eagerness for some "new blood" in the field of musical theatre. People in the "industry" (as it is sometimes whimsically called) look at their aging audiences and long for some young people to become regular theatregoers. Record companies, as well as producers and writers, look back longingly to the good old days when Broadway cast albums were number one bestsellers, bringing additional income while at the same time serving as free advertisement for the shows. Perhaps, they reason, young rock musicals will tap into the market of top pop hits and bring in all of those zillions of kids who pack the stadiums for their favorite rock groups.

Rent is an interesting case in point. Following as it did on the untimely (but extremely dramatic) death of its talented young writer/composer Jonathan Larson, and buoyed by the Pulitzer Prize, it is the unquestioned "hot ticket" on Broadway as of this writing. It will be fascinating to see whether or not it will open the door to more rock musicals by and for young people. It will make the financing of such shows easier, and once financed, the shows can be produced. Then we will see. My own feeling is that the old devices of plot and character are still the essentials, as useful to the creator of musicals as legs are to the dancer or vocal chords to the singer. If the rock scores are built upon these foundations, and if they don't allow themselves to become too convoluted and indulgent, then there is a good chance they may become a permanent addition to the musical theatre form.

To contradict much of what I have been saying, I must add that the longest-running Broadway musical of all time (as of this writing) is *Cats*, which is totally nonlinear. But I would hasten to add that *Cats*, though plotless and rocky, is anything but undisciplined. It is as if *Cats* had taken some of the best aspects of both the Rock Musical and the Concept Musical and put them together to make a stylish theatrical event. The word "event" was important to both *Hair* and *Cats* (and to some extent to *Rent*). Especially in a time of higher and higher theatre prices, people seem to want to leave their homes and tv screens only for an "event," something spectacular and memorable.

In a category all by itself is *Bring in 'Da Noise, Bring in 'Da Funk*. It is a dance show, but not in the traditional sense. It is a Concept Musical, but not in the traditional sense. It is not even a musical in the traditional sense of the word. It is an actual breakthrough into a new kind of musical theatre, one of the very few that I can remember in my lifetime.

As I understand it, the show came about because George C. Wolfe, the playwright, director, and new head of Joseph Papp's Public Theatre in New York, wanted to create a production built around the unique talents of Savion Glover, the extraordinary young dancer-choreographer who has almost single-handedly reconceived the possibilities and parameters of tap-dancing, turning it from the elegant sophistication and showy athleticism of Fred Astaire and Gene Kelly to a forceful, contemporary expression of black exuberance and anger.

Together Wolfe and Glover conceived of a musical evening which through tap-dancing would relate the history of the black experience in America, beginning with Africa and the slave ships and going right on up (or down) to the street music and the "funk" of today.

Now, this is an extraordinary concept for a musical. It is far more ambitious in scope than most book musicals and it bears little resemblance or none whatsoever to the revues and variety shows which, although they might have

The Uncle Huck-A-Buck Song from *Bring in 'Da Noise, Bring in 'Da Funk.*

a connective theme and specialize in dance, have almost always been designed to provide light entertainment and little else.

Having made this daring plan, which was unusual in its audaciousness as well as its seriousness, the two creators, Wolfe and Glover, did something even more amazing. They pulled it off. They brought their vision to life onstage in a totally new and dramatic way, providing an evening of humor and passion and extraordinary vitality. Indeed, I know of no other musical experience on Broadway in which the audience is brought to the same fever pitch of excitement and sheer joy. And although the great musicals have always been able to produce this group euphoria to some extent, in this case there is the added excitement of being present at the birth of something innovative and totally contemporary. I think the response must have been something like that at the first performances of Clifford Odets's *Waiting for Lefty* back in the 1930's, when the young people in the audience felt that, at last, *their* voice was finally being heard.

Can *Noise/Funk* form the basis for a new musical theatre? I don't think so. It is too special, too particular to the specific talent that conceived it and brought it to life. Yet I believe that George C. Wolfe is the one person working in the theatre today who has the skill and the daring to create a new musical form for our time. As I mentioned earlier, he is a respected playwright, with a knowledge of the possibilities and pitfalls of writing for the stage. In addition to that, he is a true theatre man, a showman, an expert of "the bill." Look at the "put-together" of *Noise/Funk*. Someone had to conceive the bill: What follows what? How long, how short? How loud, how soft? How much talk, and when? How much singing, and when? How much humor, and where does it fall? When do the lights go up full and when do they fade to black? Do the numbers "button" for applause or do they segue into the next beat? All of these elements are exquisitely achieved in *Noise/Funk*, and despite the pleasures of the serious sub-text and the emotional impact it conveys, an enormous part of the success of the show is based solidly on those old verities of vaudeville which shape the event and give it its contours and form.

If George Wolfe is one of the few people capable of shaping "the bill," he is also one of the rare directors with an instinct for the daring, "big" dramatic effect, as evidenced in *Angels in America* as well as *Jelly's Last Jam*. It remains to be seen if he is prepared to devote himself to musicals or whether he will continue on his present course of dividing his time between writing, directing straight plays, and theatrical management. But in my opinion, if there is a likely candidate for seriously advancing the form of the American musical, Wolfe is the one.

Sung-Through Musicals

In many ways this is the most interesting of the recent developments. It is certainly the most popular. Under the expert aegis of Cameron Mackintosh, shows like *Phantom of the Opera*, *Les Misérables*, and *Miss Saigon* have become the most popular and the most profitable theatrical productions, not only in England and America, but all around the world. The weekly financial grosses for these musicals, both on Broadway and on the road, are simply astounding. Every one of them draws seven or eight hundred thousand dollars each week at dozens of venues. And of course this doesn't include London and Paris and Berlin and Tokyo and South America and the Scandinavian countries, et al.

What are these phenomena? Are they truly a new form? Well, yes, in fact, they are. Or, more accurately, they are an amalgamation of many previous forms into a new form. First of all, they have rock-oriented scores. Second, they have borrowed much of their "put together" expertise from the American musical. Third, they rely heavily upon the traditions of European opera. Thus, they blend the "schmaltz" and the sheer "bigness" of traditional opera with rock sensibilities and Broadway know-how. No wonder they are successful. For the first time, the opulence and the "grandness" of grand opera are mixed with a contemporary sound and marketed with showbiz sophistication.

Are these behemoths then the future form of the musical? Well, maybe. There is no doubt that the combination mentioned above is a potent one, one that will be around for a long, long time. On the other hand, there is a downside to all this grandness, and that is the very real danger of over-complexity and, worse, of flatulence. Of all the creations of the American musical, none is more important, in my opinion, than the American song form. I am talking here of good old aaba, of Verse-Intro, Chorus, Chorus, Bridge, Chorus, with possibly a Tag.

There is a very real danger in the "sung-through" musical of losing this powerful, simple song form (the basis for all the great American show songs) and having it replaced by meandering and ungraspable complexity.

The Small Musical

Years ago, before we had written *The Fantasticks*, my partner Harvey Schmidt and I wrote a number for one of Julius Monk's revues in which a rather threadbare actor sang a song called "Mr. Off-Broadway," part of which went as follows:

> I've played in every kind of house.
> In every kind of hall.
> I once played Cinderella

In an empty shower stall.
The stage was kind of slippery,
But I mean, we had a ball!
Off-Broadway Melody!

Give my regards to old Off-Broadway!
Remember me to Sheridan Square!
Tell all the gang at Jan Hus Auditorium
That I will soon be there!

And so forth. Little did we know that our brief comedic comment would go on to become something like our own trademark.

Off-Broadway began primarily as an outlet where actors could practice their craft and be seen by critics and producers. Many of the most notable Off-Broadway successes in the early days were revivals of plays that had failed, often unjustly, in the Broadway environment. Such was the case with Tennessee Williams's *Summer and Smoke* and Eugene O'Neill's *The Iceman Cometh*, both of which had closed quickly on Broadway and both of which were enormous hits Off-Broadway.

Later, in the natural course of things, some musicals were added to the Off-Broadway agenda. And later still, two of these musicals became very successful. One was the Brecht-Weil *Threepenny Opera*, which had run for only twelve performances on Broadway in the 30's, and the other was the Kern-Wodehouse-Bolton *Leave it to Jane*, which had indeed been a success at the tiny Princess Theater in 1917, but which had not been revived in New York since.

It was during this period (*The Threepenny Opera* was in its fifth year and *Leave It to Jane* in its third) when *The Fantasticks* opened. Since then, many musicals have chosen Off-Broadway instead of the Great White Way (now more accurately a rather grimy gray). Some made the choice because they could not get financing for Broadway. Some (like *A Chorus Line* and *Sunday in the Park with George* and *Once on This Island*) used Off-Broadway as a way station on the road to Broadway. And some actually welcomed the opportunity to experiment with an alternative kind of theatre, a musical form which was not just Broadway shrunk but a new approach entirely.

It is too early to know what will happen to these "mini-musicals" in the age of *Cats* and *Miss Saigon*, but I have reason to believe that there is a real hunger for an alternative form, for unamplified sound, and for more personal interchange between performer and spectator. At least, I hope it is so. I, with my "little Latin and less Greek," have made up a motto for what it is that we are seeking: "Di Minimis, Moltimis." "Out Of Little, Much."

In Summation

It is clear that the musical theatre is changing. No one knows where it is going. Perhaps it is going not to one place but to many. That would be healthy, I think, just as the search in itself can be healthy.

For a long time, we had an accepted format, which meant that no one had to spend much time experimenting with the basic structure. All efforts could go into perfecting the work itself, just as Shakespeare didn't feel the need to change the theatrical conventions of his time. His theatre worked. He knew its limitations and its possibilities, and he was free to concentrate on other matters, like character and philosophic thought and mastery of language.

I'm reminded of a story about the theatre at the University of Texas. When I was a student there, we had very limited theatrical facilities. (Maybe that's why I like Off-Broadway so much.) But later on, after my time, when the Drama Department became more established, new theatre space was built as part of the new drama building. It was someone's idea to make the new theatre adaptable to just about everything. Not only could any part of the stage be raised and lowered by machinery, but any part of the auditorium could do the same. Thrust stage, proscenium-stage, theatre-in-the-round, high, low, this way, that way. Indeed, I rather imagine that the most difficult and challenging job of each director was to come up with a new and exciting way to use this new, flexible space.

Then one day a curious thing took place. The earth sighed, as sometimes the earth is wont to do, and the foundation expanded or shrunk or shifted just a bit. And the machinery stuck. Whatever the facility was set up for at the time became the only space and arrangement available. From then on, until some bright engineer finally figured out how to shift it all back years later, the directors and the designers had a different sort of challenge. This was the space. These were its limitations. And the job was suddenly to find the possibilities hidden within the limitations—to study the restrictions as a great sculptor studies a piece of marble, flaws and all, searching for the secrets of release and freedom.

Thus it was for Shakespeare in Elizabethan times; thus it was for writers of musicals after Rodgers and Hammerstein; and thus it will be again. In the meantime, we have no choice but to be explorers as well as practitioners, to discover and set the limitations which will provide us our own discovery and release.

Part II:

Putting It Together, Taking It Apart

6

Getting Started

How do you make a musical? Well, there are several ingredients that are essential.

First of all, you have to find a partner. Possibly more than one partner. It depends on what you want to do. Sometimes the writer of the book is also the writer of the lyrics. That is a good thing because if the person can do both, it reduces the chances for confusion—for conflict of approaches. Sometimes the composer of the music is also the author of the lyrics. That, also, is a good thing. And for the same reasons. Sometimes, but very, very rarely, the composer of the music is also the writer of the lyrics and the author of the book. That is a bad thing. Why? I don't know why. It just is. It is too much for one person to carry. And it is too much to expect of one person's talents. God, after all, gives with one hand, but he takes away with the other.

And there is another reason. Sheldon Harnick, the talented lyricist whose career goes from "The Boston Beguine" in *New Faces of 1952* on through *Fiddler on the Roof* and beyond, tells a story about his partnership with Jerry Bock.

Their first Broadway show was called *The Body Beautiful* and people were very "up" about it—so much so that B.M.I. arranged a big opening night party at Sardi's, complete with balloons and decorations. A large crowd of well-wishers gathered after the opening night to eat and drink and celebrate the expected triumph.

Around eleven o'clock or so, Sheldon began to notice that the crowd was thinning out, and thirty minutes later it was gone completely. Vanished. What had happened? The answer, of course, was that the first reviews had come out, and they were not good. There is nothing that can clean out an opening night party like a bad review in the *Times*. It's amazing how people know it, but they all do. Nothing is said; at least, nothing obvious. But somehow the odor of failure penetrates the perfume of the premiere, and everyone slips quietly out into the fresh, clean air of the New York City streets.

Anyway, by twelve o'clock, Sheldon and Jerry had heard the bad news. And there they sat, along with their wives, the only guests left in a restaurant room filled with warm champagne and half-eaten hors d'oeuvres. According to Sheldon, he decided at that moment never to work without a partner. At least there would be someone with whom to share the misery.

I sympathize and I concur.

How do you find a partner?

There is no practical answer for that. You seek one out. You search for one. You send out signals, like an animal in heat. Places to look? In college—that is a good place. Many partnerships began there. Ours did. Others, as well. If not in school, then around theatres—theatres where they do musicals. Be around theatres. Be around theatre people. Put the word out. Seek and (maybe) you will find. Some schools have training in musical theatre these days where they actively pair up students as partners. Large cities (especially New York) have musical theatre workshops where people find partners.

How do you know when you have found "the one"? Again, that is almost impossible to answer. How do you know when you've found "the one" in sex, in marriage, in whatever? "Chemistry," says Sky Masterson in *Guys and Dolls*, and that seems as good an answer as any.

Based on my own observations, I would offer the following pointers, which have served Harvey and me well for forty years or so (but which may not apply to you at all).

1. Find someone whose taste in shows is similar to yours. Not in art. Not in clothes. Not in lifestyle. But in actual theatre experiences. If you consistently find that you are excited, or bored, by the same shows, it is a good sign. If you consistently disagree, you will probably have trouble working together. (You'll have trouble enough; no need to add to it.)
2. I think it helps if you clearly have distinctly different talents. I cannot write music. I never could, not in a million years. Likewise, Harvey is not a lyricist or librettist. I admire what he does. I respect it. I cannot exist as an artist in the musical theatre without it.
3. Find someone to whom you may convey your honest feelings. Even harder, find someone you respect enough to accept criticism from.
4. Don't get too close, too personally close. Keep your partnership businesslike. Don't "crowd" each other. Don't socialize together too much if you can help it. If you have any success in your chosen field, you will be thrown together all of the time. Keep space. Don't wear out each other's welcome.

5. Make decisions together. On matters of business and artistic policy, you must agree. You have to agree. If you don't agree, then you still have to. You have to work it out. If you can't, you shouldn't be partners. In the domain of the other person's talent, you have to let that person have the final say. Thus, if Harvey and I disagree about a certain lyric, we are free to discuss it—even to argue and harangue. But, ultimately, that decision will be mine. The same is true of Harvey and the music. He listens to what I say. I listen to what he says. But the music is ultimately his just as the lyrics are ultimately mine.

The book is another matter, for it is more than just the dialogue. The book is the lay-out, the structure, the "breathing" in and out from large to small, from solo to chorus. The book is also the theatrical style, the "concept" which will frame and inform the visual elements and the staging. In short, the book is something that concerns lyricist and composer as well as the librettist. It is here where the different views of the various partners can often be most contentious. And it is here where agreement is most essential.

Having found a partner (or partners), you have to: Find a "property."

This is only slightly less difficult than finding a partner. This "property" can be an original book, or it can be an adaptation of an existing work. If it is an original, then you have my blessing—but not, I'm afraid, my help. You will have to go elsewhere, to a playwright, possibly. I have been trying for over thirty years to create original musicals and on one or two rare occasions I have actually accomplished it. (I even did it once to my satisfaction.) But it is not a natural gift of mine. I tend to get lost in the plots and the characters, to lose sight of the overall, which is the most important thing in a musical. Therefore, I spend most of my time these days working from adaptations. And I continue to work on originals on the side, recognizing that, with my limitations, it will probably take anywhere from three to five years to work one out properly.

If you decide to do an adaptation, try if possible, to find something in the public domain. Barring that, try to find something that isn't too "hot" a property. It takes a lot of money and time and aggravation to secure the rights to a "hot" property. You will have to compete with others who may be better established and thus more powerful than you. Even worse, you may have to compete with the "property" itself. If you musicalize *A Streetcar Named Desire*, for example, you will have to compete with vivid memories of the play and the film.

Never attempt to make a musical out of something (especially a well-known something) that you are not sure will be enhanced, even improved substantially, by being in musical form. A few years ago the producers Peter Neufeld and Tyler Gatchell came to Harvey and me asking if we would be interested in making a musical of Thornton Wilder's play *Our Town*. We were flattered, but uncertain. It is a great play, a play which is an established classic, and which has had an enormous influence upon our work. (Much of *The Fantasticks* is homage to *Our Town*.) So we told Peter and Tyler we needed some time to work with it, to think about it, to see if there was something we could bring to it which would enhance rather than diminish its power. Or, as we put it rather more bluntly, we didn't want to go down in history as the people who screwed up *Our Town*.

Our Town as a musical is fraught with dangers. First of all, the addition of songs can easily make it seem too sentimental, and that is death for a play which is all too often misunderstood as being sentimental in the first place. On the other hand, it can also become pompous, especially if one goes the operatic route, with Wilder's simple, terse prose being turned into operatic recitative. We had to be sure we could find the musical "tone," the language which could keep the wonderful, understated simplicity of the original and put it in lyric and musical form.

Second, we had to see what, if anything, we could bring to the "book," the structure, the "put-together" which could possibly enhance the original and make it more available to a present-day audience. We wanted to keep most of the elements of the great scenery-free original (talk about a concept!), although we did envision the possibility of using some sort of projections, not as scenery but as illustration, throwing them onto a screen which would be frankly acknowledged as a stage device, just as the stepladder and the trellises were in the original. We also envisioned the possibility of a piano, placed at the side, with the Stage Manager often beside it, speaking or singing. We thought of it almost as a backer's audition type of thing, which would begin with speaker and piano, and then grow and come to life as people and instruments and lights are slowly added.

And lastly, we had a vision of the point of view. As we studied the play, it became more and more clear that it was not really so much about small-town America as it was about Time—the passing of Time, the use of Time, what we do with the brief Time that we are given. There is no small-town America now. At least, there isn't much. The rural populations are shrinking, and those few that are left are a short distance from the ubiquitous mall. And everyone has *television*. The small-town America that Wilder wrote about is now too apt to be simple nostalgia, a nostalgia about a period which has been done to death in musicals (such as *The Music Man*, *Hello, Dolly!*, *Oklahoma!*, and dozens of others). By trimming the original down to make room for the music, we could also remove some of the material about small towns of long ago and focus more on the importance of the passing of Time, a theme which will never seem dated or sentimental.

Only after we had studied the project for a long time were we sure that we had a unique and personal vision of *Our Town*, and only then did we feel that we could add something to the original play by turning it into a musical. It was at that point that we agreed to accept the assignment.

Whether you choose to do an original or an adaptation, there are certain things to look for when searching for a property.

Obviously, the original source should be something that excites you—something that moves you—to tears, to laughter, to terror. If it doesn't move you, if it doesn't really have an emotional effect on you, forget it; you don't have a chance.

You should look for some sort of manageable length. *War and Peace* is a little difficult to put on a musical stage, or any stage. Although—I don't know—you may have a vision as to how it could be done. If so, you might as well give it a try. But you will have to begin by realizing that enormous size is a major (*the* major) problem you will face, and you have to be sure that your proposed solution doesn't "steal" too much from other vital matters, such as getting to know the characters, getting to care about them, etc.

You should look for a reasonably-sized cast. Again, that is a problem that can be met with sufficient ingenuity. Any problem can. Any problem can be solved if you feel the original piece strongly enough and if you realize the scope of the problem fully and if you have the skill to pull it off.

Finding "the problem" is a very important thing when working on a musical. Almost every musical has one. Indeed, almost every musical has more than one. But aside from the inevitable host of small problems and difficulties, there is usually a major problem, a structural problem, and if you can locate this early enough and deal with it realistically you will save yourself lots of grief (and time) later on down the road.

Years ago, Lore Noto, our producer from *The Fantasticks*, decided to do a musical based on Marjorie Rawlings' book *The Yearling*, about a young boy in the Florida Everglades who befriends a young fawn and raises it until, inevitably, it has to be released to return to the wild. Lore loved this story. He even named his youngest son after the boy in the book. Lore threw his own considerable efforts as a producer into bringing the project to life. He lined up a talented composer and lyricist who wrote a memorable score. He collaborated on the book because he had such a vivid vision of the characters and the story.

When he asked Harvey and me what we thought of the project, we felt compelled to ask: "But how are you going to do it? How are you going to do it with the deer and all the other wild animals that are a vital part of the story?" Lore was nonplussed. "What do you mean?" he would say; and though we tried to explain our doubts, he simply did not grasp them. If you need a deer, why, that's all right. You get a deer. It's as easy as that.

Many months later, when the show was in deep trouble in its out of town tryout, we were again consulted, and again we stated the same question: "What are you going to do about the deer?" to the same baffled response, "What do you mean?" For whatever reasons, Lore, and his many talented co-workers on the project, could not seem to grasp the fact that bringing a real deer onto a stage for a few moments at a time while it stared bewildered at the strange surroundings and pooped on the floor would not summon up the absolute magic of what the deer was in the book.

And yet, this was the essential problem, the structural problem. If you couldn't perceive it and come up with a stageworthy solution, the piece would be doomed to failure, as indeed it was. Not that Lore was not bright. He was, and is, a shrewd and dedicated man, capable of fervent and courageous convictions. But in that particular instance, neither he, nor his writers, nor his director, nor apparently anyone else could grasp the essential problem. And if you can't grasp it, you sure as hell can't solve it.

To know what would make a good musical, it is first necessary to ask the question, "What Is a musical?" Is it a play with music? No. I guarantee you, it is not that. If you take a play and insert songs into it, you will have a play with music. And it will be a bastard form, a disaster.

What then is a musical? The dictionary says it is: "a theatrical presentation involving characters and plot (or sometimes theme) in which the major points are realized in musical form." That is a good start. I would add a few other factors I feel are normally part of a good musical.

1. The form must be sufficiently presentational to allow the characters to sing and sometimes to sing directly to the audience without seeming strange or out of place.
2. Each musical needs a distinct overall shape, or form. This shaping will be the major objective of all the participants in the creation.
3. The book, or libretto, must be short enough to allow room for the musical sections.
4. Thrust. The musicals that "work" are powered by some sort of thrust, a feeling of motion, of moving

forward.

5. Pace. Musicals have, or should have, a feeling of pace—a quicker, tighter feeling than a play. Everything in a musical, including the pace, is economical.
6. Simplicity. For the above reasons, musicals have a simplicity and a boldness that distinguish their form. The big picture, the overall, the bold strokes—these are what count in a musical.
7. Finally, one of the most important things to look for when searching for a musical source is a subject that lends itself to poetry as much or more than it does to prose. Don't misunderstand me. By poetry I don't mean mellifluous language or arcadian bowers. But I do mean language that is colorful in some way, and expressive.

Presuming that one has by now acquired the perfect partner and a thrilling project upon which to work, the next step is to "lay it out" and begin writing.

7

BASICS

Perhaps the hardest thing to know about any musi cal you plan to write is: "What is it about?" This may seem obvious, but believe me, the obvious things are often the most difficult to see.

Let me give you an example. When Jerry Bock, Sheldon Harnick, and Joe Stein had the idea of doing a musical based on the Tevye stories of Sholom Aleichem, they acquired the rights and wrote the complete score and libretto before approaching a producer or director. Hal Prince at first turned them down because he felt the material was not "his cup of tea." He suggested they show it to Jerome Robbins, who immediately loved the idea and accepted the directorial assignment.

However, as soon as he became the director, Robbins began to convene frequent meetings with the writers. He felt that they had dealt only with the surface of the stories, and he wanted to get to the core. He put to them the simple question mentioned above. What is it about? They answered that it was about a Jewish milkman with five daughters who live in Russia and get caught up in a pogrom and— But Robbins interrupted. "No, no," he explained, "I know the plot. What I want to know is, what is it about?"

Finally, after much thought, they came up with this answer: "It's about tradition, a way of life that is about to be dissolved forever." And that was the secret that he had been seeking, the center, the unifying force which held it all together and made it relevant, not only to that community at that time, but to all people at all times. (And, incidentally, it led to a new opening number, "Tradition," to make it clear.)

Comden and Green tell a similar story about *Wonderful Town*. Then there is the famous tale of how *A Funny Thing Happened on the Way to the Forum* was bombing during its Philadelphia tryout and Jerry Robbins, called in to "doctor," told Stephen Sondheim to throw out the Opening, a pretty romantic ballad called "Love Is in the Air," and write something to let the audience know that the show was going to be a knockabout farce. The new number, "Comedy Tonight," was brilliantly staged by Robbins, and immediately after it was added, the audiences ceased being confused and became convulsed with laughter, and Robbins' well-earned "genius" reputation received another jewel in its crown.

It would seem that a good part of Jerome Robbins' famed magic at fixing musicals consists of simply asking the writers what it is about and then putting the answer clearly at the top of the show to get things started on the right track. Of course, there is a great deal more to it than that, but this does illustrate how structural and functional it is to begin work with the most simple and basic questions.

Don't misunderstand me. A play is not a mathematical equation, though some writers treat it as such. I personally don't believe it is necessary to begin work on an original play or musical by stating the premise, as recommended in many books on play construction. I don't think it works like that. A play or a musical can begin with a moment, or with a character, or with a fragment of a plot. It can begin with a mystery, an image, something which haunts you. It can begin for no reason at all that you can clearly understand. And sometimes you have to follow its lead to find out where you are going.

But at some point in the process, you must know the answer: What is it about? And, in the case of a previously existing work which you are planning to turn into a musical, you must know the answer right away, before you start on the piece.

There are three things that you have to consider when you start to work on a project: Premise, Plot and Concept.

The Premise is what it is about. Not its plot, but what it is really about, as illustrated in the story of Jerome Robbins and *Fiddler on the Roof*. This is the most important thing of all, and often the hardest to discern.

Plot is, well, plot. It is the events that occur, and the sequence of the events, and the conflict in those events and their eventual resolution.

"Concept" takes a bit of explanation, for "Concept" is a fairly new concept, at least in the musical theatre. Utilized initially to describe the musicals resulting from the collaboration between Hal Prince as director and Stephen Sondheim as composer-lyricist, the term has also been applied to *Cats* and *A Chorus Line* and other musicals with a "nonlinear" format, as well as *Dreamgirls* and *Nine* and *The Will Rogers Follies*, shows in which the "concept" is as important, or even more important, than the story.

Let me now turn to a work of ours, *The Fantasticks*, to illustrate the difference between Premise, Plot and Concept, as well as to make a few points about looking for the overall shape—the form—of a piece you are conceiving.

The Fantasticks is based (very loosely) on a French play, *Les Romanesques*, written by Edmund Rostand when he was twenty-four years old. The plot of the original play involved two fathers who build a wall between their homes and pretend to feud in order to get their romantic and rebellious youngsters to fall in love. The essential elements of this plot are retained for the musical.

The premise of *The Fantasticks* is entirely different from the premise of the original play. It is stated in the opening song, "Try to Remember:" "Without a hurt, the heart is hollow." And it is stated even more explicitly at the climax of the second act when the two young lovers, hurt and disillusioned, sit on either side of the stage, facing forward, and El Gallo stands center above them, forming a triptych, and says:

> There is a curious paradox
> That no one can explain.
> Who understands the secret
> Of the reaping of the grain?
>
> Who understands why Spring is born
> Out of Winter's laboring pain?
> Or why we all must die a bit,
> Before we grow again?

So, though the plot of *The Fantasticks* is taken from *Les Romanesques*, its premise is quite different. It is, in its own romantic, lightweight way, about the agrarian religious concept of dying (or being hurt) and being born again (becoming stronger or wiser for the pain endured).

What about the "Concept"? We had one. Not only did we have one, but our concept became the guide which influenced every writing decision that we made. On the simplest level, the concept was this: We decided to have the little play, the "parable," acted out on a simple platform stage by a small band of actors in the manner of a commedia dell' arte troupe.

More than that, we decided to make our musical a celebration of the presentational stage devices which were, at that time, almost totally absent from the American theatre.

We decided to have a Narrator who could speak directly to the audience, setting the scenes and explaining the story and moving us forward whenever necessary, dispensing with the "realistic" exposition and time-consuming realism of the modern stage. We decided to utilize the "Invisible" Prop Man from the Chinese theatre to assist in creating scenic effects by such simple suggestions as holding up a cardboard moon or sprinkling confetti to evoke the image of rain or snow. We decided to keep the musicians in full view. We decided to have direct address to the audience. And we decided to have the whole thing written in verse.

In other words, our concept was to put actors on a simple platform and, with the use of presentational stage devices *and the imagination of the audience*, to see if we could tell a story of growing up that would touch people, would make them laugh and cry.

After we had these three things firmly in mind, the writing of *The Fantasticks* was relatively easy. For years we had tried to turn the little Rostand piece into a large Broadway musical in the Rodgers and Hammerstein mold, but it was terrible. Not only did we not have at that time the requisite skills to write in the R & H manner, but the delicate little Rostand play simply could not stand all the heavy-handed, semi-realistic treatment. Finally, when we threw it all out (up) and chose instead to break the rules and write for the kind of theatre we loved, we then discovered our premise and our concept. And after that the bulk of *The Fantasticks* was written in three weeks.*

*If you are interested in a more detailed description of how this took place, I suggest you check the Thirtieth Anniversary Edition of *The Fantasticks*, published by Applause Books, in which it is all outlined in a brief history called "Trying to Remember."

Two more notes about the creation of *The Fantasticks*: First, any time you can come across a "big" idea, a "structural" idea, you will find it very helpful in clarifying your work and holding it all together. For example, we realized that we wanted the two acts of *The Fantasticks* to be different. Act One is about "Illusion." Act Two is about "Disillusion." Therefore, we decided that we would set Act One in Moonlight and Act Two in Sunlight. As the second act begins, the Narrator reverses the cardboard moon, revealing, on the other side "the Sun." "Moonlight." "Sunlight." Very simple, but very clear. And very theatrical, as well.

Tom Jones as the Old Actor and James Cook as the Indian in *The Fantasticks*. Japan, 1988.

Second, a brief word about "inspiration." In *The Fantasticks*, there are, in addition to the Mute, two characters who have no counterparts in the original Rostand play. They are Henry and Mortimer, the Old Actor and the Man Who Dies. They came from—where? I have no idea. They just appeared. I was writing something else, and out they popped, like Athena from the head of Zeus. They appeared in Act One, on their own, and wrote their own dialogue. I had nothing to do with it at all. My writing wrist simply followed their instructions. It all lasted about ten minutes, maybe twenty, and then they were gone.

Later, when I tried to summon them back for a necessary reappearance in Act Two, they would not come. Try as I might, they simply refused to come back out of the box. They had had a wonderful exit at the end of Act One, and they seemed determined not to spoil it with a convenient re-appearance in Act Two.

Thus it was that I had to make them up for the second act. I had to come up with something, so I summoned up the image of the fox and the cat in Disney's film *Pinocchio*, and I tried to model the Old Actors' second act appearance on my memories of that. I then added plenty of doubletalk and heavy rhyming to make them seem more amusing than they in fact really were. (I had learned long ago, from Julius Monk and the revue days, that, when in doubt, one should always have lots of rhymed couplets whizzing by very fast so that people would think that something terribly witty was being said.)

In short, I managed to more or less pull it off. It wasn't really the Old Actors, the ones who had come to me so mysteriously that wonderful morning long before, but it was good enough. It was professional. It would get by without hurting the show or even destroying the memory of the Old Actors in Act One. And only the most discerning would notice it at all, and maybe they would be discerning enough to forgive.

By all of which I mean to say—that one should value inspiration above all else. It is truly a gift from the gods. But when the gods are not in a giving mood, you'd better have some professionalism to pull you through.

I sat in recently at an ASCAP Workshop, where young writers tried out some of their songs from works in progress in order to get feedback from their peers. And the one bit of advice I gave which seemed to me to be of any value was this: You have to be able to write a ballad. If you want to work in the musical theatre, you have to be able to write a ballad. And it must be pleasing, and distinctive, and not corny, and not too much like other ballads, while at the same time being simple and easy to grasp.

Also, you have to be able to write a comedy song, a song that will actually make people laugh. If you can't write a comedy song, you can't write for the musical theatre. Lastly, you must be able to write a "hallelujah" song, a rhythm or "up" song, which will make people tap their toes and jiggle their knees and want to get up and move. If you can't do that—well, you know the rest of the line.

A ballad. A comedy song. A hallelujah number. These are basics. You have to learn to do them. If you can't do all three of them, you can't play. Give up. Or keep going until you do learn how.

There are lots of other things you will have to learn, of course. Lots and lots of things. Beyond those, there is the whole question of finding your own voice, of bringing your own individual stamp. But first, you have to learn the basics. You have to acquire the skills. And if you can't do these basic things, don't break your heart. Give it up. Choose something else.

8

Writing in the "Standard" Form

You will notice that when I speak of a "standard" form I am very careful to put the term in quote marks. Why? Because there is no true standard form. The shape of the musical is always changing. Still, there was a time when the Rodgers and Hammerstein format came close to being universally accepted by almost all writers for the American musical stage. Indeed, this form (or formula), in addition to being the basis for most of the classic musicals of the 40's and 50's and 60's, is still the format most in use today. It is still very effective. And, like a painter learning perspective and design before branching out into the uncharted world of modern art, every aspiring writer for the musical stage needs to have a basic grounding in the R & H form before striking out on his or her own.

I have already written in Chapter Four about the characteristics of this "standard" form, but now I would like to write about it in a more detailed and personal way. That is to say, I would like to take the two musicals Harvey Schmidt and I have written in this form and describe in detail how we approached the basic material and how we laid out the overall structure, looking to see if we could find the way to break the shows open, to make them "musical."

First, let's take *110 in the Shade*.

A year or so after *The Fantasticks* opened, we were approached by N. Richard Nash to see, first, if we were interested in working on a musical of his play *The Rainmaker* and, second, if we had ever written anything in a "Western" mode. The answer to both questions was yes. I had been a fan of the play ever since I saw it on television the night before I was discharged from the army, and Harvey knew the piece from the excellent movie starring Katharine Hepburn and Burt Lancaster. As for the "Western" part, we are both from Texas and felt we knew this world and these people. In addition, we had done some work on a musical that is set in Texas, and we were able to play parts of that score for Mr. Nash (who, from now on, I will refer to as Richard).

Everything seemed to be coming into place; Richard would be doing the book and Harvey and I writing the score. But before Richard reached a final decision, we wanted to make sure that we all saw the piece in the same way. For that reason, Harvey and I suggested that we write out a basic point of view and treatment, giving our vision of the play as a musical and indicating several places where we thought songs might occur.

Looking at some of these early notes may be a good way to demonstrate how one approaches turning a play into a musical. So:

The premise of the play was pretty clear. It is that dreams and romanticism are necessary to bring fulfillment into our lives. The plot was also very clear. And very expert. The exposition is deft, and often funny and touching even as it is informative. The various stories all dovetail and grow and develop together. There is a build, a climax, a resolution—all the things you long for in a good plot.

We had a clear premise, a wonderful plot, strong characters, and, as an extra dividend, a wealth of beautiful, colorful language, especially in the speeches of Bill Starbuck. We had almost everything you could want in a musical except for songs and dances and—a musical form.

Even though the play was richly supplied with the things you look for in a musical (including a certain element of the Cinderella story), the form was still very much in the prose idiom popular for straight plays. Technically, we needed to take the story out of three acts and put it into two. Technically, we had to find a way to provide for some singers and dancers, since this was to be a Broadway musical in the R & H format. But, beyond all that, we had to find a way to "break it open," to move it out of the realistic confines and conventions of a well-made play and into the world of the presentational, the "epic."

First of all, we looked for a signature, a "something" that would give us an overall sense of structure, of form. The answer, we felt, was in the sun. The story is about drought. Drought is about sun. We decided that the thing to do was to take the idea of the one-day time frame mentioned in the stage directions of the play, and actually use that day to follow the progress of the sun as it interacts with the story. We would begin our day with the rising of the sun. Then we would follow the sun throughout the course of the first act as it got higher and higher, and hotter and hotter.

That decision to follow the sun led us to our next important decision, when to break the story into two acts. In the original three act form, the day ends in the first scene of Act Two when Lizzie, told that she is going to be an old maid, goes rushing out of the house. Then, in the second scene of Act Two, it is clearly night. As the stage directions put it: "Moonlight, moonlight alone, illuminates the inside of the tack room." Since we wanted to break our two acts into day and night, we decided that the place to end Act One would be right after Lizzie runs away from the others. Then, standing on a bare stage in a white dress against the flaming red colors of a western sunset, she would sing some sort of song about being an old maid. The image in our heads was very specifically Scarlett O'Hara at the end of the first half of *Gone with the Wind*, standing on the hillside with the red sun behind her, saying: "I'll never be hungry again!"

Then, we reasoned, Act Two would take place at night, when the merciless sun has given away to the softer, more romantic moonlight, and Starbuck and Lizzie make love.

This was our first structural "vision." It is the exact opposite of *The Fantasticks*, which states in the program: Act One takes place in the moonlight. Act Two takes place in the sun. However, even if we did seem to be copying ourselves, the basic value of the idea was still valid. Act One: Sun. Act Two: Moon. There is something very structural about that. Very simple. Very solid.

The next thing we felt we had to accomplish was to find a way to "break out," to escape the confines of the prose play. To accomplish this, we felt the need to get the musical outdoors.

Now, musicals can take place totally indoors, and some rare few actually do so. But the musicals that take place indoors face a problem. And this problem is difficult to explain, but very important to comprehend.

Musicals move. Not all of them, of course, but most of them. (And I would say that all musicals in the R & H mold do move.) They tend to take place in a series of scenes in a variety of locales, some indoors and some outdoors. In this, they are like Shakespeare. This sense of "movement," of a variety of scenes and locales, is part of the fabric of the American musical, and the sequencing of these scenes and locales is as much a part of the structure, the "breathing" in and out, as is the sequencing of the songs and dances. Sometimes big. Sometimes small. Yin and yang. That is the musical form.

Most twentieth century plays tend to take place in one set, and most of them are written in two or three full acts, rather than in a number of shorter scenes. Their technique is essentially the same: Set a small group of people together, slyly slip in the exposition that has brought them to the edge of conflict, explore the conflict, hit a climax, reach a resolution.

In other words, these plays begin at the point of conflict, use exposition to explain how they got to that point, and then, by a slow accumulation of details and confrontations, build up to their climax and resolution. Musicals, on the other hand, tend to lay out the whole story, opting for a series of short scenes instead of exposition. As I said, they are very like Shakespeare. Take *Romeo and Juliet* as an example. Shakespeare's version begins with a street battle between the two feuding households. Then we meet Romeo, a callow youth heartsick over his lost love Rosalind. Then we find out that Juliet is to be married to Paris and that her family is planning a masked ball to celebrate the event. Then Romeo is persuaded by his pals to go, uninvited, to this party in the enemy household. There he meets Juliet. Then he sneaks outside her balcony to see her, and they agree to meet the next day. Then they hastily get married. Then Romeo reluctantly gets involved in a street brawl and, in a fit of passion, kills Juliet's cousin Tybalt, for which he is banished from the kingdom. Lots of scenes. Lot of action. And we are only halfway through the plot.

In a modern play, the action would probably begin somewhere around this point. We would find out, through exposition, what has occurred up until now, and the rest of the time would be spent showing the desperation and eventual death of the two impetuous lovers. A musical, on the other hand, would lay it out in the way Shakespeare did. (Check *West Side Story* to see what I mean.)

Not only are musicals more like Shakespeare, they are also more like movies. They shift locale, they have a variety of shorter scenes, and they can employ a form of "montage," compressed images, to carry us forward through time and place. A notable example of this can be found in the film script Shaw adapted from his play *Pygmalion*. Alan Jay Lerner is often credited for his brilliance in "breaking open" Shaw's comedy but, although his lyrics for *My Fair Lady* are truly wonderful, the so-called "breaking open" was done by Shaw himself when he wrote the screenplay. There he could actually take us into the "squashed cabbage" environment that Eliza came from and then, at the other end of the spectrum, take us to the famous embassy ball. Along the way, he could use montage to show the slow and tedious weeks of teaching Eliza how to speak.

Let's return to *The Rainmaker*. We were fortunate in having a play that was already divided into a number of short scenes. Furthermore, it was a play that had been made into an excellent motion picture. When we made notes on how to "break it open," we went first to the screen version, where we found the train station and Lizzie's return from Sweet River. Next we searched our own youths and memories of Texas in summer, which led us to the idea of the Fourth of July and the annual town picnic. This would get us out where we could see that blasted sun. It would also give us a natural way to bring in some of the people nearby. This then was our structural contribution. We

Three early sketches by Harvey Schmidt while searching for the visual look of *110 in the Shade*, 1963.

would break the play into two acts. In the first act we would follow the sun, from its rising ("Another Hot Day") to its flaming sunset ("Old Maid"). We would set the story on the Fourth of July and use the picnic and celebration as a way to introduce the Chorus of singers and dancers (an indispensable element of all R & H shows). Then, to conclude our notes, we listed a number of places for songs and dances; and Harvey, who had been an artist before he was a composer, made a series of watercolor sketches "storyboarding" our ideas for the look of the show.

To our great relief, Richard agreed to all of this. Many of the concepts were similar to what he had in mind and others, like the following of the sun, he seized upon eagerly. I would like to add that, helpful as we may have been to him in "breaking open" the form of the show, Richard was equally helpful to us in finding the right places and ideas for songs. There was never a number we wrote that wasn't directly or indirectly influenced by Richard's suggestions and comments. It was a wonderful collaboration for all of us, one that we remember with great pleasure.

110 in the Shade was to be our first Broadway score, by the way, and in our eagerness to do it right (and in our terror of doing it wrong), Harvey and I wrote one hundred and fourteen songs before the show went into rehearsal. Our theory was that whenever the musical got into trouble out of town, we could go to our hotel rooms, order drinks and dinner from room service, turn on the television, and then come out the next morning looking exhausted, saying: "Well, we've got one for you."

Ironically, we had to write three new numbers out of town, one of them ("A Man and a Woman") put into the show so quickly that the leads, Inga Swenson and Stephen Douglas, had to come down to the front of the stage and read the lyrics from huge cue cards held up by the stage manager in the orchestra pit while they sang.

Now, leaving *110* behind, let's look at the structure of *I Do! I Do!* This musical is based on a two-character play by Jan de Hartog called *The Fourposter*, which was a Broadway hit starring Hume Cronyn and Jessica Tandy in the early 1950's and a terrible motion picture with Rex Harrison and Lili Palmer in the late 1950's.

Interestingly enough, we did not set out to make a musical out of this play, just as we had not set out to make a musical of *The Rainmaker*. In both instances, we were approached by outside sources. In this case, Harvey and I were in Italy, working on an original, when we received a call from Gower Champion saying: "Boys—" (If you write songs, you are always called "Boys," unless you are Comden and Green, in which case you are called "Kids." If you are Stephen Sondheim or Andrew Lloyd Weber, I don't know what you are called. "Boy"? "Sir Boy"?) Anyway, Gower said: "How about a musical based on *The Fourposter*?" And we thought: what a terrible idea.

Then he said: "Wait. How about a musical based on *The Fourposter*—produced by David Merrick—directed by Gower Champion—starring Mary Martin and Robert Preston?" And it began to sound better. In fact, it began to sound irresistible. So we decided to give it a try. We had no idea how it could be done, or even *if* it could be done, but it was a fascinating challenge and we agreed to spend a month or so trying to find a way to "break it open."

To understand the problem, it is necessary to first outline the play. It has only two characters, the husband and the wife, and one set, the bedroom with the fourposter bed. The play is divided into three acts, and each act has two scenes. In these six scenes, the author covers six prototypical events in the life of a typical marriage over a period of twenty-five years. (We made it fifty in the musical.) Although there is no plot in the usual sense of the word, there is a continuing development of the same two characters, and each of the scenes has a mini-plot of its own. For example, in the wedding night scene, they are both shy and inexperienced, and the "plot" concerns how they will overcome their shyness and consummate their union.

In addition to the two full-fledged intermissions in the original play, there are long pauses between each of the scenes, so the characters can change costumes and, in some instances, their make-up. In other words, the "rhythm" of the experience, from the audience's point of view, is to enter an auditorium, sit down, watch a curtain go up, see the scene completed, watch a curtain go down, wait in the demi-darkness until it goes up again and the play resumes. Very stop and start. Very prose. Very "play." Very un-"musical."

So the question became, how to take that stop-start prose play and turn it into a fluid presentational form—in other words, a musical. You cannot just put songs into these scenes. If you do that, you will have a play with music, a bastard form. Not only will the songs seem strange and out of place, they will appear to slow up the action rather than speed it up and compress it. (We did not discover it until years later, but *The Fourposter* had already been made into a musical before we were approached. I have never seen or heard this version, but from what I am told, the writers did just what I described above. They took the play and inserted songs, and the piece did not work.)

In our case, we did not approach the problem head-on. For one thing, we were still neophytes in the world of structure and analysis, and we were not clear as to how we should begin. Then again, I had been recently married and was eager to write something about this touching, ludicrous, enduring institution. Indeed, I had already written some lyric notes about marriage, and so Harvey and I decided to set out by writing a grab-bag of lyrics and melodies inspired by the idea of marriage.

I gave him a lyric called "I Love My Wife," and he set it, neither of us knowing where it would go in the show, or even if it would fit in at all. I had a title "My Cup Runneth Over with Love," which Harvey made into a nice long-line melody, which I then took back to fill in the rest of the lyric. I asked my wife to give me a list of my most irritating habits and I made a similar list of her petty faults, and these I turned into lyrics. In other words, in addition to looking into the text of the play for song ideas, we compiled a whole trunk of material which was about marriage but not necessarily about these six scenes from *The Fourposter*.

Eventually this growing mass of material gave us an idea as to how the piece might be done. First of all, we knew we could not stop and start as in the original play, pulling down a curtain in between scenes. All costume and make-up and scene changes would have to be done in a fluid manner, without stopping the show or altering the rhythm. Second, we knew that we had to somehow introduce a presentational element into the proceedings so that it wouldn't seem strange and inappropriate when the people suddenly turned to the front and burst into song.

These two considerations led us to the form we chose: namely, that we would not confine the material just to the scenes in the play, but we would continue on between those scenes with short presentational, almost vaudevillian, turns. In other words, instead of starting with the couple entering the bedroom on the wedding night, we would start with them just before the wedding. We would see just the two of them, in pools of light as we hear their secret thoughts prior to the ceremony. Then we would, in a highly stylized and compressed form, go through the ceremony itself; after which we would take them into the bedroom and the first scene.

At the end of that first scene, which we musicalized in the normal R & H way (looking for speeches or moments that lend themselves to song and/or dance), we would dim the lights on the nuptial embrace. Then, instead of bringing down the curtain and having a stage wait, we would have the husband, Michael, get out of bed in his nightgown and sing "I Love My Wife," eventually waking Agnes so that the two of them could do a happy, barefoot softshoe dance together. After that, when he gets back into bed and goes to sleep, we had her put on a pregnancy costume in view

Mary Martin and Robert Preston in the original production of *I Do! I Do!*, 1966.

of the audience as she sings "Something Has Happened."

And so on. We put our presentational bits in between the scenes, keeping the flow going and enabling us to openly acknowledge the presence of the audience. Since part of what we were attempting was a daring and original attempt to do a musical with just two people, we decided that it should be, in addition to a celebration of marriage, a celebration of performance as well—a celebration of the art of two great stars.

There was a flaw in this piece, too. (There is always a flaw.) In this case the flaw is inherent in the material. Marriage, as many of you know, is a very complex institution with an infinite variety of human emotions, ranging from deep, deep love to terrible frustration and sometimes even hate. But *The Fourposter* isn't really about that. As Mr. de Hartog said to us when we played the score for him, *The Fourposter* is a valentine to marriage, a loving and humorous and *light* treatment of a complex subject. And therein lies the rub. What we wanted—what we set out to do—was to write something that would cover the whole range of marital emotions, but what we wound up with was (and is) a valentine. A nice valentine, to be sure. And an accomplished one. But one that may well leave the discerning theatregoer asking: "Hey, but what about the other side—the dark side?"

This problem was further complicated by the necessity, in R & H terms, of having "showstoppers." It was then considered an essential element of any successful Broadway show that there be several numbers that literally stop the show by inciting prolonged applause and cheers from the audience. And this requirement was all the more necessary if one had famous stars. We managed to come up with the showstoppers, which, if I may say so, was not so easy to do in a show without a chorus, scenery, or any significant dance. But the very nature of the showstoppers (at least, the ones we could come up with) put the show more into the showbiz category and took it further away from the area of psychological exploration. In short, whenever we moved too far from the valentine, our efforts seemed as out of place as putting "My Cup Runneth Over" in the middle of *Who's Afraid of Virginia Woolf?*.

I Do! I Do! "works" and I am proud of it. It works better now than it did originally since we were able to do some "balancing" and rewriting for the excellent 1996 production at the Lamb's Theatre in New York. It manages to be a big, Broadway-type show in spite of the fact that it has only two people and one set. It is much "bigger," for example, than *The Fantasticks*, which has eight people. It is hard to explain this. The "scale" is larger. The writing is larger. It is bolder, more "socko," more "Broadway." It was great fun to do, but in my heart of hearts I think I still prefer the smaller—or if not the smaller, the more experimental—type of theatre more associated with Off-Broadway than with "On."

One of the things I wrote about in the first half of this book is the curious mix in the Broadway musical of "variety" and "legit," of star turns and storytelling. "Razzle-dazzle"—that's what Bob Fosse called it, and of course, he was a master of it. But, much as I may enjoy an occasional razzle and a furtive dazzle or two, I find I don't enjoy them unless they are connected to (and lesser than) a simple story about human beings with whom I can identify and empathize.

"*De gustibus*."

9

Experiments

In the late 1960's, with *I Do! I Do!* running on Broad way and *The Fantasticks* Off-Broadway, Harvey and I decided to do something that we had dreamed of since our college days. We rented a building, fashioned a stage, and set out to try and write a series of original musicals in new and untried forms.

The building was called Portfolio, and it was located on West 47th Street in Manhattan in the heart of the theatre district. Our stage, which Harvey designed, was a very useful and attractive variation of the Elizabethan stage, with side platforms joined to an "inner-above" and "inner-below." The building, which had once been a chapel for immigrant weddings, had ceilings high enough to hang lights, and the whole space was eminently theatrical and evocative.

We were set, we felt, to take the next logical step in our evolution. After arriving in New York, we had begun by writing sketches and songs for supper clubs and revues. Then we made our "legitimate" debut with *The Fantasticks*, which was done Off-Broadway, and for which we had done book and score based upon another work. Next, we had done music and lyrics, but not book, for our first Broadway musical, *110 in The Shade*, followed by *I Do! I Do!* for which we did book, music and lyrics, but again based upon another source. Now we were set, or so we thought, to do book, music and lyrics to an original musical which we would also design and direct.

This was known, in Greek times, as "*hubris*" (meaning overbearing pride or presumption) and was customarily followed by "*nemesis*" (meaning retributive justice or revenge). It's what happened to Prometheus: for his *hubris* he was chained to a rock to have his entrails forever gnawed by an eagle. It's what happened to Oedipus: he was forced to rip out his eyes and wander the world, forever blind. And it's what happened to us.

Drawing by Harvey Schmidt of the original stage setting at Portfolio Workshop

First of all, let me make clear that the designing and directing were not the problem. These we did well. Although I am sure that we could have profited from the cross-pollination that comes from the normal give-and-take of the rehearsal process, we were able to avoid the confusion which is all too often a part of that tumultuous time.

The problem was simply that we didn't know how to write an original musical. Or, to be more specific, since I am the one who writes the books, *I* didn't know how to write an original musical. Our careers, which had moved so smoothly, depended upon a certain set of talents which were more intuitive than learned. Neither Harvey nor I had studied "musicals," and although I had prepared myself for a career in the theatre, it was to be as a director not a writer. And now our lack of training caught up with us.

To further aggravate the problem, we felt that we could not only create original musicals, but could do them in totally new ways, with revolutionary techniques and visions. If this were not vain enough, we also felt that once we had created these new and revolutionary works, Broadway would want them. Not Off-Broadway, or Off-Off-Broadway, which would seem the logical territory for new and experimental work, but Big-Time Showbiz Broadway (with the Big-Time Showbiz Broadway royalties and the B-T S-B fame that went with it).

In short, we were naïve. And we were arrogant. And we got bashed. And hopefully, we grew. Along the way, we did create several new original musicals, some of which were pretty good, and all of which contain ideas and experiments which may be valid, not only for us and our continued search, but for other writers who may be looking for new techniques to replace or supplement the tried and true R & H format.

The first show we did at Portfolio was *Celebration*. It was an attempt to do a ritual musical with gags and a few naked girls. That is to say, it was an attempt to mix what Peter Brook called "the holy theatre," the theatre of myth and ritual, with "the street theatre," the theatre of clowns and entertainment.

For source material, I went back to the earliest use of drama that I could find, a Sumerian ritual in which the Old Year, portrayed as a burnt-out, aging tyrant, does battle with the New Year, a young hero figure, the prize being the hand of a young maiden. The New Year wins, of course; the Old Year dies, the maiden is (presumably) impregnated, and the world goes on.

We decided to set the whole piece on New Year's Eve, transferring the characters and the settings to the present time. Harvey began to collect and create a multitude of masks that were truly unique works of art. Starting with some cheap plastic masks from the local novelty store, he began to paint, glue, gild, and add delicious geegaws. On one of the masks he fastened two whisk brooms on either side for ears. On another he pasted hundreds and hundreds of buttons of all colors and shapes. On another, he took Dixie cups, cut out the ends and pasted them on for eyes.

While this was going on, a friend of ours, Charles Blackburn, let us have a whole roomful of colorful costumes he had created for various productions. There were rags and tatters from *The Threepenny Opera*, a bizarre group of monsters from *Doctor Faustus*, long robes from Shakespearean productions, top hats and tails, and even a complete gorilla outfit, to which we added a pink tutu and a diamond tiara. It was a treasure trove, a gold mine, and it fit in perfectly with the antic but theatrical atmosphere around Portfolio.

We opened *Celebration* at a "midnight matinee" on Halloween 1968, at our Portfolio theatre. The response was sensational: overwhelming, ecstatic, socko. Our brief showcase run was limited to a handful of performances, but

Ted Thurston as the Old Man at the New Year's Eve party in *Celebration*, 1969.

Michael Glenn-Smith as the Young Boy surrounded by Revelers with placards of city faces.

before they were over, we had acquired a Broadway producer, a Shubert Theater, and all the money we needed to produce the show on Broadway (which wasn't much, because we already had the cast and the physical production and some of the orchestrations). Three months later we opened at the Ambassador Theatre to wildly mixed but mostly negative notices.

Celebration—an attempt to create a ritual musical "with laughs and a few naked girls."

I have a funny picture (funny/sad) taken at the opening night party. Harvey had slipped on the ice and broken his leg the first week of rehearsal, so he was still in a wheelchair. I had thrown my arm out of joint during the rigors of a picture call, and my arm was in a sling. Our producer, Cheryl Crawford, had been nearly killed by her embezzling associate, who tried to smash her skull with a gilded picture frame. And there we sit in the photograph, forever captured at the moment of our disaster—Harvey in his wheelchair, me in my sling, and Cheryl in her head bandage. Had we been healthier, we might have dragged ourselves over to a window of the Times Square Building, where the opening night party was being held, and flung ourselves into the street below. Instead, we survived. And unlike *Celebration*, which closed after a hundred and nine performances, we continued at Portfolio, trying to find out what had gone wrong and what we had to do to learn to do it right.

Looking at it now, from the hindsight of a quarter of a century, I know that the score and the dialogue and the characters were all right, but that the plotting was weak and the entire point of view unclear. And I also know that if we had taken our experiment to Off-Broadway, where it rightfully belonged, it would have had a healthy run and a much more active afterlife.

What experiments, then, did we develop at Portfolio which are worth passing on to someone else? There are two basic techniques which I would like to discuss with you. The first has to do with the use of principals as chorus. In an original musical called *Philemon*, we hit upon the idea of keeping the entire cast on stage throughout the show. At first glance, this seems like *The Fantasticks*, where, inspired by the Piccolo Teatro production of *A Servant of Two Masters*, we have the actors, when not actively in a scene, sit at the side, often with their backs to the audience. But in *Philemon*, we went one step further. We decided to have the cast face front and watch the drama being enacted and, when the occasion arose, *to sing along with the principals*.

In other words, instead of just sitting around waiting as in *The Fantasticks*, the principals could become a singing chorus when needed. In *The Fantasticks*, we have a cast of eight but no musical numbers involving more than three or four people, but now, with *Philemon*'s cast of seven, it was possible to have a much fuller choral sound with the entire company all singing at the same time.

Of course, it became necessary to establish some sort of premise to make this possible. In the case of *Philemon*, the premise was easy. Six members of the cast share the duties of Narrator. They appear at the top of the show, line up facing the audience, and sing. Then, as the music continues, the actors quickly put on their costumes and introduce the clown Cockian, who doesn't ever break the "fourth wall." He is trapped in time, like a fly in amber. It is his story and he is "in" it. Only the others address the audience and step in and out of time as they alternate between playing the people in Cockian's story and communicating directing to us as an audience. In a way, it is like a reverse image of *The Fantasticks*, where El Gallo can step in and out, speaking directly to the audience, while the other characters remain "in" the story.

Years ago I had gone with Gower Champion to see Jerome Robbins' exciting ballet of Stravinsky's *Les Noces*. Robbins had placed a rather small wooden platform downstage center. On either side of it were several grand pianos, which played the score, and in the back, standing on a series of bleachers, was a chorus of singers, who sang the words. Then, as the ballet proceeded, Robbins audaciously tried to "squeeze" the dance patterns into the tight confines of that wooden platform downstage center.

I was struck. The image haunted me for years. The wild passion being compressed into that small space hit me in a very personal way, underscoring my own feelings about raw passion being made more powerful by being "caged" within the strict confines of poetry (or lyrics). Also, as you may have guessed by now, I am a sucker for a wooden platform on a stage, especially if it is downstage center.

We worked on *Philemon* for a long time. We did four complete and separate versions before we finally found the form of the finished work. (In fact, we did it so often that Jay Harnick suggested we change the name of our theater from Portfolio to The New York Philemonic.) And as we continued to work on the piece, I continued to be haunted by the memory of that Jerome Robbins ballet.

Finally, the obvious connection became clear to me. We would have a platform, a wooden platform, and it would be down center. And it would be in blazing hot light. And our story would take place there, or around there, with our leading character, Cockian, trapped in time. The others would be around him, on bleachers or platforms, in the half-light, watching. Sometimes they would comment on the action, sometimes they would sing, and sometimes one or two of them would step forward into the light where they would become part of the story being told, after which they could return to their perches, to watch the drama unfold.

And that is what we did. The principals became "chorus," and our very small cast, being freed from the necessity of realistic explanation, filled the small theatre with rich, full sound. We didn't have to "explain" them.

Once we had made our premise clear, the audience accepted their continued presence and their frequent singing. Just as in *The Fantasticks*, when the show is playing well, no one notices the piano player sitting right by the actors and facing the audience. If all is playing well, the audience is quite capable of "losing" these other elements and entering into the "reality" of the story. The audience, we have found, can do anything, just as long as it is clear what the "rules of the game" are. It is not necessary to "explain" a chorus, to "justify" them, if you are clearly in a presentational framework. It is not necessary, as in the R & H mode, to say, "Oh, here come the kids from down the road" or whatever, in order to bring in "happy villagers" to augment the singing and dancing.

The concept of the platform. In this early version of *Philemon*, at the Portfolio Workshop, Cockian is in the "hot center" while the other principals, also doubling as chorus, comment from the sidelines.

Later, as we worked on our original musical *Colette Collage*, we followed the same path. Again, there was the "hot" platform downstage center. In this case, it was Colette's desk, which was the center of her universe, and which opened out at various points to become a music hall stage or a bar in St. Tropez, or a bed. (Frequently a bed.) In this case, Colette was the central character, the narrator, and the rest of the ensemble were her memories, her "ghosts." And, sure enough, they gather at various levels in the shadows at the sides, watching and listening. They become the ghostly citizens of her tiny village of St. Sauver when she gets married. They become the decadent denizens of the Parisian demimonde, the performers in the music hall, the summer lovers in the south of France.

In this York Theatre production of *Colette Collage*, Colette's desk served as the "hot center," opening up to be a bar, a bed and a musical hall stage, among other things.

When needed, they step forward into the story. The "Principals," Colette's mother, her various husbands, and her homosexual confidant, move forward into the story as required. The "Ensemble," three men and three women, play a variety of different roles throughout the seven decades that the story encompasses. All of them may sing together, as "chorus," whenever required by the demands of the music.

In *Grover's Corners*, our musical version of Thornton Wilder's *Our Town*, we have done the same thing.

Rather than seeing the characters enter as the story unfolds, as in the original play, now we see them gathered in the shadows from the very beginning. Again they are memories from another time. Again they watch as the story unfolds. When they are involved, they move forward into the action. When not involved, they watch from the shadows, joining in the singing when required.

In this recent sketch by Harvey Schmidt, we continue to explore the possible uses of the platform for the upcoming production of *Grover's Corners*.

There are shows for which this technique will not work, of course. But there are many instances, especially with an imaginative stage piece such as *Our Town*, that this use of principals as chorus can increase the effectiveness of the choral music and at the same time underscore the theatrical excitement possible when one breaks away from the old ways and asks the audience to join in creating a new theatrical experience.

The other technique which we have tried over the past few years has to do with the intertwining of music and spoken words. There is nothing new about underscoring, of course, but I am talking about something more than that. I am talking about the structuring of a complete scene around a piece of music, around a song.

In the Thirtieth Anniversary tour of *The Fantasticks*, starring Robert Goulet, some elements of the Portfolio platform were added to expand the presentational possibilities, as in this first act "Happy Ending" tableau.

But first, let me begin by restating my belief in the traditional popular song form. It doesn't necessarily have to be thirty-two bars. It doesn't necessarily have to be aaba, even Verse-Chorus, Verse-Chorus, but it does have to be *graspable*. It has to be compressed. It has to be clear. It has to be emotional, or funny, or revealing. Just as the theatre itself is a compression of many emotions and events into two hours or so, the song form I am speaking of has to be a compression of a powerful and clear emotion or idea into three or four minutes, or less.

On the other hand, musicals are not as simple as they used to be. Influenced primarily by opera and to a lesser extent by the free form of rock songs, composers and lyricists have a desire to expand the vocabulary of the modern musical beyond the traditional popular song form. Thus we have the sung-through musicals such as *Phantom* and *Les Miz* on the one hand, and the increasingly complex "pointillism" of Sondheim and his many imitators.

Partly in rebellion against the long-established (and too easily anticipated) R & H format, there is a desire to make musicals less simple and more challenging, not only in their songs, but in their stories and characters. I personally think this is a good thing. If the musical is ever to "grow up" and become more than just a happy-go-lucky reassuring pop massage, it must be able to take on stories and characters that are more complex. And it must be able to bring them to life in song forms that are more flexible than the old thirty-two bar aaba. There must be room for recitative, for long-line and diffuse musical elements. Having said that, I hasten to add that these complexities must not replace the popular song form, but be an addition to it.

For Harvey and me, the solution to this challenge has been in development for a long time. We have always been interested in music composed especially for the spoken word. Back in the old Julius Monk revue days, we did several pieces which were "spoken arias," long, spoken narratives, usually in verse, sometimes in rhyme, where the words and the music were composed to go together, just as in a regular song. Later, in *The Fantasticks*, we used this technique on a number of occasions, most notably in what we call the "glen speech," a summoning of the senses composed for harp and spoken voice.

For some reason, it didn't occur to us to combine these spoken sections with the songs of *The Fantasticks*. These were done in the usual way. That is to say, you got to a cue, what Richard Nash calls a "gozinda," then you did your song, after which you did a "gozeoutta" to get you back into the scene. Sometimes the songs were solos, sometimes duets or trios. Sometimes they were reprised or made to include a musical section for dance. But usually they were just "songs," song, button, applause, back into dialogue.

The same thing was true of *110 In the Shade* and *I Do! I Do!*, our Broadway-type shows, and even *Celebration*, our first "experimental" musical. But then, as we continued at Portfolio, we began to realize that we could state a theme musically, with a "regular" song; then, without stopping, we could continue the music as it changed into something more complex, or possibly as it became part of a "spoken lyric." Then, again without stopping, we could segue back into the basic theme, the song in standard "pop" form.

For example, in the opening of *Philemon*, the six people who narrate and play the principal roles in the story line up across the stage and sing directly to the audience:

CHORUS

Within this empty space
There is nothing we cannot do.
We can seek to create something great
From the past
Or search for something new.

Within this empty space
There are secrets to be revealed.
There are things that we know in our bones
To be so
And emotions we long to feel.

Flesh!
If we wish it, there are pleasures of the flesh.

Just as much as we desire.
Clowns!
Being human, well of course there will be clowns,
And if laughter makes us tire

Tears!
In the end there will be bitterness and tears,
And the purifying fire.
The purifying fire...

Within this empty space
There are worlds to be opened wide.
Come along, come with me, unafraid, you will see
We will find ourselves inside.

From the horror of hell
To a state of grace,
All are here, waiting here,
Within this empty space.

(NOTE: This song is in a standard, or traditional form, aaba with a coda at the end. But now, instead of stopping, as we did with "Try To Remember" at the opening of *The Fantasticks*, the music continues. It changes configuration, but it continues over the same basic beat, as Cockian appears. He does not seem to see or hear the others as they speak over the music, dividing the lines among them.)

CHORUS

This man is Cockian.
A clown.
Fall down!

(A rim-shot on the drums as Cockian does a pratfall.)

He lived in Antioch,
A distant capital of Rome.

His stage:
A wooden platform
In the middle of the street.
His song:
A simple one.
Example:

COCKIAN

(Sings)

Oh, gimme a good digestion
And something to digest.
If you provide some bread and wine
It needn't be the best.
Just keep the people eating.
There'll never be unrest.
Gimme a clown to laugh at,
A lady who's undressed.
Oh, gimme a good digestion
And something to digest.

(COCKIAN continues strutting and doing rooster imitations in the hot light on the wooden platform as the others speak from the shadows.)

CHORUS

Observe him closely.
He is dead.
He has been dead for almost seventeen hundred
years.
His bones lie buried beneath the sands
Of what is now called western Turkey.
His painted clown-white flesh
Has slid away and vanished:

Rejoined the elements that gave it birth.
His jester bells are silent.
His comic phallus is forgotten.
His jokes are blown, like pollen,
Through the empty skulls
Of those who one time watched him.
All dead.
Whatever truth there is—
Whatever quick perception—
Whatever ability there is to feel,
To leap across the precipice of Time—
All this exits within ourselves.

(And they sing:)

Within this empty space
There are worlds to be opened wide.
Come along, come with me,
Unafraid, you will see
We will find ourselves inside.

From the horrors of hell
To a state of grace,
All are here, waiting here,
Within this empty space.

We can see in this example not only the use of principals as chorus, but the extension of a regular aaba song into a small "block," encompassing spoken words and other melodies, all contained within the basic framework of the original song. Later, in *Grover's Corners*, we used this technique almost exclusively throughout the entire show.

For example, *Grover's Corners* begins with a song by the Stage Manager called *Our Town*. After he sings it, the music continues "under" as he speaks, introducing us to the town and the people. This segues into a series of musical recitatives between the townspeople as the day begins, and then to more musical underscoring as the Stage Manager has one more section of talk. Finally, at the climax, the Stage Manager and all the rest sing the Our Town song together, going for a big vocal climax at the end.

In the Wedding Scene, the principal theme, a long-line ballad entitled "I Only Want Someone to Love Me" is introduced, then broken up by speeches and short snippets of song and recitative, then returned to again and again until it finally concludes with everyone singing together in full, majestic harmony.

During Act Two, as we go to the final Graveyard Scene, the Stage Manager sings a song called "Time Goes By," a rather wistful ballad about the changes wrought by Time and about the acceptance of our own inevitable death. It concludes: "And this moment—now —is the only one we own. Time goes by. Time goes by. Time goes by."

The music continues as the Stage Manager talks about the hill where the graveyard is located; this moves into a series of small "songlets" as the dead people sing the epitaphs that are on their tombstones. Music goes back to the basic theme of "Time Goes By" as the Stage Manager does the powerful speech about the dead being "weaned away" from life, waiting for the eternal part of themselves to come out clear. The Stage Manager and the dead people all sing the end of the song together, with the group dropping out at the very end, so that the Stage Manager can conclude quietly on his own.

And there you have it: Blocks of music built around one basic, simple, solid *song* with a memorable melody and a clear lyric. Then this block is opened up to contain speeches and bits of scenes and songlets or recitative.

The advantage is that the score is made up principally of some ten or twelve strong, simple, *graspable* songs, as in the days of the great musicals of the past. But now these basic songs are expanded to include sections of more musical and lyrical complexity.

10

Lyrics

I have tried, during these notes, to focus on the overall, the structural, rather than the specific. This is partly due to my belief that it is the overall view which is most important in the formulation of a musical, and partly because I tend to be suspicious of formulas which are too specific. I have seen books which confidently lay out such topics as "How to write an opening number," "How to insert reprises," etc., and inevitably these tomes point to this or that great musical from the past to illustrate how such things are done. But such "rules" make me nervous. They limit the possibilities. And they are often *too* related to the past.

As far as I can see, an opening number must get the audience's attention and must set in motion the machinery of the play. If it can set an atmosphere, create a mood, that is good. If it can tell us something about character, that is better. And if it can tell us something about the premise, that is the best of all. But then, to go from that into suggestions as to how to do this seems to me fraught with dangers. The how-to is the exclusive domain of the creators. The best a "teacher" can do is to point out the problems and the possibilities and leave the solutions up to the artists.

I do think it is possible to teach something specific about the art and craft of lyric writing, but I think that it is extremely difficult to do it "long distance," without the personal involvement and interaction between teacher and student. So much of lyric writing has to do with the mouth. With the mouth and the ear. With the making of sounds, the "feeling" of sounds inside the mouth—the way certain things bounce off the back of the upper "lid" of the mouth; the way certain vowels sound with certain notes of music; the way consonants pop and twitch and click the teeth and tickle the tongue. These are things you have a feeling for or you don't. I'm not sure this feeling can be taught, but if it's there to begin with, it can be developed. It can be developed by singing. And you don't have to sing well. In fact, I sometimes wonder if singing too well isn't bad for a lyricist; it focuses too much attention on "tone," on "placement," on the production of sound.

Many of the best lyricists don't sing "well." That is to say, they don't sing with beautiful tones (or always on-key), but they do have a feeling for the expression of words with music. It's almost as if, not being able to produce those beautiful tones themselves, they try to compensate by filling the notes with expressive, "singing" words. Oscar Hammerstein could not "sing." Neither could Ira Gershwin. Neither can Stephen Sondheim. But all lyricists "sing" when they are writing. We all mouth words. We all sing in the privacy of our work places. Sometimes we sing out loud, but more often we sing silently, mouthing the words we are working on with the melody at hand and hearing in our heads the glorious sounds as if they were coming from a wonderful singer.

If you are working on a lyric to an already set piece of music, then you "sing" your words to that. You play the music on the piano if you can, and on the tape recorder if you can't. And often you simply play the music in your head. You "hear" the tune. In fact, you hear it all the time, just as one "hears" a melody that runs round and round your brain (like a pretty girl).

If you are working on an original lyric, not to an already written melody, then you still need to sing. You make up a melody of your own. It doesn't matter how awful it is. No one will ever hear it but you. (Although sometimes when I have written an original lyric, Harvey asks me to record the tune I was hearing in my head, and then I have the embarrassing task of singing my miserable little melody into a tape recorder and listening to my wobbly voice instead of the mighty melody and the clarion sound I was hearing in my head.)

Lyric writers are mumblers. They are mouth-people. They enjoy making sounds for the sheer pleasure of producing them in the mouth. My two young sons are mouth mumblers. (Perhaps all kids are, at a certain age.) They love to just sit around and make up sounds, elaborate mixtures of vowels and consonants and rolling "r's" and guttural "g's" and high, whining "n's" or "m's," like some insane ersatz language, like Sid Caesar speaking bogus German on the old *Show of Shows*, like Danny Kaye rattling off pretend Spanish or French, like high "holy-rollers" shouting out in ecstasy in the "unknown tongue." As I said, probably most kids go through this. Lyric writers never outgrow it.

One other thing I would like to mention before getting down to some specifics. Lyric writing is normally done in pencil on a page. Never with a typewriter. Never with a computer. Rarely with a pen or a marker. The ink would dry out before you get to the next word. (NOTE: One should never make rules. After writing the above, I was reminded that Sammy Cahn wrote only on the typewriter, and Sheldon Harnick tells me that he has a fountain pen that he favors, partly because of the way the words stand out when written. Aside from my silly restrictions, my point remains the same: lyric writing is often a very slow and measured process.)

If the theatre is an act of compression, and musicals are a further compression, lyric writing is the most compressed of all. There is a tendency these days to let lyrics (and songs) drone on and on, meandering this way and that, but the real art (and the real craft) of lyric writing lies in the act of compression. To get an emotion, or an idea, or a revelation, and squeeze it down into its most compact and graspable and memorable possible form—that is the challenge and the joy of lyric writing. Thus, there are very few words involved, and every word, every juxtaposition of words, is of extreme importance. Every "and" and every "but" and "the" is weighed with extreme care. Every word, every phrase, is repeated over and over again (in the mouth, in the "ear") to see if it "works," to see if it sounds "right," to see if it is the best word or phrase that you can possibly get. This can be hard, very hard, especially if you want the end result to sound simple and unpremeditated.

But...back to that blank page and that pencil. When writing a lyric, it is best not to pin down things too soon. The page, or pages, should remain "open" to possibilities. You need, when working on a line in a lyric, to put it down, and then leave room to try out several lines which might follow it. You need room at the side of the page to put down rhymes that occur to you, or phrases, or words—half-formed images, germs of ideas. You need to keep it loose and free and "floating" around the page; at least, in the beginning. Later on you will have to pin it down more specifically. You will have to discover the form, the rhyme pattern and the shape and length of the verses. You will have to decide whether or not to have a bridge: to structure the song aaba or abab or even aaa. (Our two most successful songs, "Try To Remember" from *The Fantasticks* and "My Cup Runneth Over" from *I Do! I Do!* are both structured in this curious aaa form.) You will have to decide if you want an intro or a coda, or possibly if you want to write in a free form, with no set pattern at all.

But even at this stage you should be cautious about pinning down the page too much. The more typed and "set" it is, the more official and finished it appears—and the more like "Literature," the more like "Poetry." And this kind of thinking, even if it is only subliminal, is to be avoided at all costs. Never forget that a song lyric is to be sung. What it "looks" like means nothing. What it "sounds" like means everything.

This is largely true of plays, as well. Sometimes I think it would be better for drama schools never to give out neatly printed scripts for the plays they are about to produce. Better to have something scruffy, something scribbled on and scratched out. Maybe they should even hand out handwritten pages, in no particular order, so the prospective actors would have to figure it out by themselves. The results would be time-consuming, but I think the students would learn something in the process, and I think it might make the process of creating something for the stage more understandable, and more fun, than just looking at those cold, pristine pages of print.

When learning to write lyrics, one should write lyrics, just as when learning to act, one should act. If you can write both lyrics and music, that's great. You can work by yourself. If you can't compose, then you should try to find someone to write with. And if you can't find someone to write with, you should do the best you can on your own. Write original lyrics and practice singing them to your own made-up tunes. And work with "the greats." Get some musical selections from Offenbach and Tchaikovsky or any other famous (dead) composer who has clear, strong melodic lines, and write lyrics to that. Then sing them and see if they actually do "sing," if they are pleasurable in the mouth. Then tape them and listen back and try to remove yourself from the process long enough to judge whether or not they are clear, whether or not they are memorable. Then work them over again. Rewrite. Make them better.

Rewrite standard lyrics. Or try to. Take some of your favorite songs from your favorite musicals, and sing them to yourself. Sing them over and over. Check out the words as you sing. Can you improve them? Can you change them at all? Try to keep the same meaning and feeling of the song while actually changing some words in the process. Try to figure out why the lyricist made the choices that he did. Undoubtedly he, or she, considered other options, many of them. Why did he, or she, decide on the final words in the song?

Break songs apart. Again, taking songs you like from shows you admire, lay them out on the paper so that you can dissect them. What is the basic form? What is the key idea? How is it captured and made clear? What about it is most distinctive, most original? Though you may have to type out the words to better analyze the form, always sing along in your mind when you are making artistic judgments about songs.

Later, when you get more experienced, you should do this same sort of analysis with complete scores of shows that you admire. How many songs? What is the form of each one? What is the "type" of each one? How much variety is there, and how is it achieved? How many ballads? How many comedy songs? How many solos? How many duets, chorus numbers, dance numbers, production numbers? Etc., etc., etc. And don't forget to indicate whether each song contributes to the "story," the forward movement of the plot, and if so, how so. Be around musicals. Go to see them as often as you can. (It may be too expensive to buy seats all the time.) Be in them if possible. Help out backstage. Hang around. Get the "sound" in your ear, the rhythm, the "feel," and not just for the songs, but for the whole score, the put-together.

Writing songs, like writing anything, may begin in an infinite variety of ways. A phrase comes to you, a "feeling," a theatrical moment, and you follow it where it leads. But for most songs—at least, most songs of the standard form—you need very soon to find a key phrase or idea that ties it all together, that pulls it into shape. Often this phrase may be in the title of the song. Sometimes the phrase comes at the top of each chorus and sometimes at the end. When doing your homework with those favorite songs, look to see what is the unifying phrase or idea.

Sometimes the key comes in a lyrics-first song, as in "Much More" in *The Fantasticks*, in which the girl sings of her passionate dreams of extraordinary things, with each section of lyric ending with the phrase: "Much more!" and with the whole song ending:

> Perhaps I'm bad,
> Or wild, or mad,
> With lots of grief in store,
> But I want much more
> Than keeping house!
> Much more!

Much more!
Much more!

Sometimes the key phrase will come music-first, such as "Try To Remember" from *The Fantasticks*. We actually had another song written to open the show, a song in which the Bandit-Narrator sings: "Follow along with me, Follow the song with me, Back to a world that is easy and slow..." inviting the audience to come back to a more romantic time, a time of innocence and youth. The idea seemed right and the song was acceptable, if not extraordinary in any way. But then I heard Harvey playing this melody he had composed (for fun), and it was so beautiful, so memorable, so right for our show, that I resolved to try and "set it" for the opening number. Accordingly, I asked him to put the music down on tape, and I began to listen over and over, trying to feel out the form, trying to find the "key" that would unlock the door to the structure.

Interestingly, the key for me was not the opening line or the eventual title but the little two-note "catch" which echoes at the end of each of the three choruses. Da-dum. Da-dum. Da-dum. Thinking of the other number we had already done, I decided that the *mot juste* for this phrase was "follow." And that became the key to the song for me. There are three choruses. Each one ends with this "da-dum," or "follow;" therefore the preceding portion of each chorus should lead up to that "follow." Come along with me. That's what the other opening had said. Listening to this new music, which didn't fit that phrase, I decided upon "try to remember," which did fit the new music well. Try to remember—that was the beginning, not only of the first line, but of almost every other line at the top half of each chorus. In other words, try to remember this and try to remember that and try to remember the other, and if you remember, then follow. And thus the structure of the lyric fell gradually into place. I decided to have lots of interior rhyming and many off or near rhymes to add some complexity to the simple, haunting melody and the rather repetitious aaa form, and I decided to change the last chorus to "Deep in December" to give some variety and to make the point of the song, and the show:

As for example, Chorus One:

> Try to remember the kind of September
> When life was slow and oh, so mellow.
> Try to remember the kind of September
> When grass was green and grain was yellow.
>
> Try to remember the kind of September
> When you were a tender and callow fellow,
> Try to remember, and if you remember,
> Then follow.
> Follow, follow, follow.

And the last chorus:

> Deep in December, it's nice to remember,
> Although you know the snow will follow.
> Deep in December, it's nice to remember:
> Without a hurt the heart is hollow.
> Deep in December, it's nice to remember
> The fire of September that made us mellow.
> Deep in December, our hearts should remember,
> And follow.

When we first played "Try To Remember" for our mentor, Dr. Sirmay at Chappell Music, a very Viennese musicologist who had been instrumental in many careers, including Cole Porter's, he expressed dismay. "Vere's de bridge?" he kept asking over and over in his heavy accent.

"Try To Remember." Jerry Orbach and the original cast of *The Fantasticks*. "Vere's de bridge?"

"Vere's de bridge?" Well, we never did find the bridge, but it all worked out to everyone's satisfaction, even Dr. Sirmay's.

Sometimes a song may be a "mixture," a combination of lyric-first and music-first. For example, when we were working on *I Do! I Do!*, I jotted down a great many song titles and/or phrases, a grab-bag of ideas or images having to do with marriage. One of these was "My cup runneth over with love," borrowing the phrase from the Bible and altering it slightly to fit what I wanted to say. I thought no more about it and returned to my primary task, which was to come up with as many lyrics as possible about the honorable estate of marriage.

A week or so later, Harvey played me a melody he had written to that scrap of a lyric. It was a simple but very powerful song of three choruses, aaa, each chorus ending with the phrase: "My cup runneth over with love." And then, what made the song distinctive was the fact that the word "love" was held for a long, long time, a full twelve bars, growing stronger and more powerful as it swelled out over a very distinctive counter-melody played in the accompaniment. It was terrific. Very powerful. Immediately "grabbing." And, as it turned out, it was also hell to "set" lyrically.

As I said, the form of the song was aaa, with no intro, bridge, or coda. Just those three choruses. And each chorus was just four lines long. And the fourth line of each chorus was already set to the same basic phrase: "My cup runneth over with love." That meant that the song was twelve lines long and the three key lines were pre-set and there were only nine lines left to write. To someone inexperienced in the ways of lyric writing, this might seem easy. But, in fact, the opposite is true. The more lines, the more freedom; the more words, the more chance to try for something original and distinctive. Conversely, the fewer lines and the fewer words, the more compressed and restricted the challenge becomes.

So here was my problem. We had an interesting title and a wonderful musical setting, but to save the song and make it "work," I had to come up with something distinctive and memorable that was at the same time very simple and unaffected. The form of each of the three choruses was aabb, and all of my key rhymes had to be with the word "love," which has only a handful of rhymes to begin with, and that handful has been worked to death, as in "dove," "glove," and "above."

I couldn't do it. I tried and tried. I nearly went crazy trying to make up new words that would rhyme with "love," words that somehow must have escaped the editors of my rhyming dictionary. I had managed to come up with one chorus:

> Sometimes in the morning,
> When shadows are deep,
> I lie here beside you, just watching you sleep.
> And sometimes I whisper what I'm thinking of:
> My cup runneth over with love...

This wasn't bad. The "of" rhyme wasn't very distinctive, but it also wasn't very distractive. It slid by okay, and it all fit well with the music. And the long, sung "love" sort of overpowered the whole thing anyway and made the lyric seem acceptable. As I struggled with the second chorus, I finally made a momentous (for me) decision: Screw it. Forget the "love" rhyme. Ignore it. Every time I tried to come up with something distinctive for that spot, it stuck out like a sore thumb. So I would forget the rhyme. I would downplay it, and move on to the meat of the matter as unobtrusively as possible. Thus, Chorus Two:

> Sometimes in the evening, when you do not see,
> I study the small things you do constantly.
> I memorize moments that I'm fondest of.
> My cup runneth over with love...

The third and final chorus had a key change before it,

Mary Martin and Robert Preston sing "My Cup Runneth Over" in the original production of *I Do! I Do!*

and it clearly needed something to make it as distinctive lyrically as it was musically. Being still blocked by those old "love" rhymes, I decided to rely instead upon assonance, resembling sounds coming down on the strong downbeat which was stressed in the last chorus.

> In only a moment we both will be old.
> We won't even notice the world turning cold.
> And so, in this moment, with sunlight above,
> My cup runneth over with love.

Forget how it looks on the page. That means nothing. If you happen to know the song, say or sing the words with the music. If you don't know the song, simply say the lyric, stressing the heavy iambic pentameter beat: In *only* a *moment* we *both* will be *old*. We *won't* even notice the *world* turning *cold*... And so forth. These near-rhyming sounds running through the body of the chorus give it a richness which the aaa structure of the song and the aabb structure of each chorus tend to prohibit.

Where do you find "ideas" for lyrics? Obviously, when working on a musical, you find ideas in the basic subject matter, the book. Look in the book. Possibly underline some line or image in the text, or put an asterisk beside it. Look for the actual title of the song that might fit into this particular spot. Look for the phrase or line or word which sums up the idea and is captured in a speech or possibly even in a stage direction.

Look particularly for the *obligatory* number, the speech or phrase or idea that seems to demand to be musicalized.

Second, you can look for song ideas that are suggested by the text, or implied by it, but which are not actually in the book as written. Such ideas are very valuable, perhaps even more valuable than those spelled out in the text, because these are ideas—or, more accurately—*emotions* which you have after experiencing the text. This is not just something experienced by someone else. This is *you*. And you are as important, or more important, in this process than the original creator. You are not just a midwife. You are now the new parent, mixing your creative genes with those of your spouse, the original creator.

Get a notebook. And a pen. Put it alongside the text and as you are reading, write. Not a lot. Not yet. A word, perhaps. A phrase. An image. Get as close to your subconscious as you can. If something takes off, if your wrist starts writing, follow where it leads you. Never stop when your hand is writing instead of your mind. On the other hand, you shouldn't "set your mind" for long essays here—just feelings and impressions. You don't want to interrupt the overall flow of the material as you are encountering it.

Then, when you have finished reading, and writing your notes, add to them. You can write more "fully" now, but still, don't "organize" yet. Don't try to give things form. Just get down on paper any thoughts and feelings that the material has brought out in you.

In addition to the book, another valuable source for ideas may be the book-writer. I normally do book as well as lyrics for our shows, so I don't have much personal experience in this. But you can see it makes sense. Have a bull session with the librettist. Have two. Have a dozen—have as many as you need. Toss out ideas. Discuss scenes and characters and moments. And be alert. Listen. Listen for that idea, that phrase, that jumping-off point.

As with the book-writer, so with the composer. Again, a give-and-take of ideas and titles and places for songs can be most valuable. Speaking for myself, a little of this goes a long way. But this is strictly a matter of taste. Harvey and I exchange notes and ideas at the top of the process and periodically along the way, but there are other writers who work together constantly while doing a show. They go over every lyric, every word together and argue and discuss it.

Sometimes other collaborators can be helpful, too. Principally this will be the director, but sometimes it can be the producer. Of course, a good director or producer is wise enough not to try and help with a lyric or even a lyric idea. Instead, he—or she—will ask the right questions, will pinpoint the areas where something is not quite right. Then the wise director or producer will let you take the suggestion and set about solving the problem.

But suppose you are not working on a musical and you still want to write songs for the fun of it, or for a revue or a nightclub act or a recording, or simply to learn more about the art and craft of lyric writing. Where do you find ideas in that case?

Well, like most "arts," like most "professions," like most activities of any kind in life, it involves a "mindset." You have to get "tuned in" to the process.

I don't know how this happens. It just happens. It is natural. It is the way our species functions. Before I had children, I never saw children. Now I see them everywhere. I never miss one.

I'm not much of a photographer, but my partner Harvey is both a marvelous painter and an excellent photographer. He sees light and color in a totally different way than I do. He sees a girl in an orange dress and he sees how she is framed against a white window with a blue frame around it.

I, meanwhile, will register what the girl is saying much more than he. Not just the context, but the cadence. Often he won't hear the girl at all. He will be hearing music—and seeing images of color and form more brilliant than any available in the immediate vicinity.

I, meanwhile, may be mumbling. I may be lining up vowels and consonants, sometimes for their poetic effect, more often just for their sounds, the hypnotic pleasure of their sounds.

What do accountants dream about? What do they see pass before their inner eye in those soft moments before they fall asleep? Sex? Maybe. Domestic tension? Very possible. But I feel sure there are times, many times, when little dots and dollar signs and decimals go dancing around —adding up, dividing, multiplying like protoplasm.

What do athletes dream about? And dancers? And gamblers?

As I said, it involves a "mindset." It comes when you spend a lot of time pursuing a subject or a field that you care about very much. And it can, like any form of concentration, be developed. Take a certain amount of time each day to consciously think about lyrics. Think of titles. Look around you. Look for song ideas. Listen to what others are saying. Is there anything being said that might make a lyric? Maybe it won't be a clear idea or a title, but rather just a phrase, a certain rhythm or grouping of words. Carry a small notebook. Jot down ideas. Consciously form the habit and in time you won't have to think about it all. It will be part of your routine.

Sometimes you can get ideas from the public domain. I have done that several times. In Carl Sandburg's long poem, *The People, Yes*, there is a section of folk sayings and proverbs, and I have been there more than once. For example: "Why did the children put beans in their ears, when the one thing we told the children they must not do was to put beans in their ears?" This I borrowed and rephrased for "Never Say No" in *The Fantasticks*. Also, from that same group of sayings, I did a lyric called "Wishes Won't Wash Dishes" for our obscure, "male menopause" musical, *The Bone Room*. From the Anonymous section at the back of *Bartlett's Familiar Quotations*, I borrowed "Give me a good digestion and something to digest" for *Philemon*.

Other writers have done similar things. "There but for you go I" from *Brigadoon* is an ancient saying. "I'm always true to you, darling, in my fashion" from *Kiss Me, Kate* is a Cole Porter reworking of a saucy Restoration poem. "Speak low, when you speak love" from *One Touch of Venus* is taken from a very obscure, almost throw-away line in *Much Ado About Nothing*. You can use quotations from the Bible, from Shakespeare, from Mother Goose—thoughts or sayings which have already been expressed *and com-*

pressed. Then you may take them and expand them, or change them, or modify them. It can be an impetus, something to get you started.

Sometimes when writing, it helps to read—to read comic poets, for example, when you are working on comedy songs. Not to steal (not *necessarily* to steal), but to get the mindset. I used to read Phyllis McGinley when working on *I Do! I Do!* I often read Edna St. Vincent Millay, just to help my mind-set. I don't often listen to songs or read other lyricists for my mind-set, nor do I necessarily read anything at all. Still, sometimes you need fueling. While working on *110 in the Shade*, I listened to many Folkway records from the West, just to tune my "ear," to help my mind move back to another time and place.

Plus which, you never can tell. Maybe there will be a little word or two, a phrase, you can "borrow," or at least adapt.

Of course, the first question that anyone will ask if they find out you write songs is: "Which comes first, the lyrics or the music?" And the stock answer to that stock question is usually: "the book." But beyond that truism, it is my own feeling that there is no "logical" way which is better than the other. Lyrics first is good. Music first is good. A mixture of the two can also be good. It is largely a matter of temperament. Harvey writes melodies on his own. Many of them are good. We would be mad not to use them if they seem to fit the mood and the moment and the character involved.

For what it is worth, our working process is this: We examine the basic source material which has been suggested to us, or which we have suggested ourselves, as a possible basis for a musical.

We each put down our impressions. First, whether the book or play or film "hits" us, whether it moves us in some way. Second, we note what the problems are and how we might possibly solve them. And lastly, we each put down our vote as to whether or not we want to work on it.

If we decide that we do want to give it a try, we either make an agreement with the owner of the rights, or the producer who has brought it to us, or we may possibly wait until we explore it further before we make a final commitment. In either case, we begin a series of meetings where we share our initial impressions about what could be musicalized, followed by any thoughts about which sections might be best approached music first or lyric first, or perhaps explored by both of us separately. After we have discussed all of this thoroughly in daily sessions over a period of several weeks, we split and go our own ways.

Harvey immerses himself in the basic material and he begins to write music, not necessarily for any spot, but just musical impressions, emotional reactions. Although these musical impressions are normally without lyrics or even a lyric idea, they are almost always in some sort of song form, as opposed to more diverse and extended musical composition. Harvey likes to journey to the source when he is writing these melodies. When we started working on Colette long ago, Harvey rented a house in France for the summer, visited Colette's village, got up at 4 AM as she did and wandered the same fields as she. He read Colette's novels. He looked at paintings and photographs of the period. And he wrote melodies, thirty-eight of them, to be exact, and almost all of them were exciting and eminently useable. Some had titles which he would make up just to identify the tape cassette. Harvey's title "Mr. Fascination," for example, wound up being "Something for the Summer" in the show. Sometimes the titles would indicate the area where the songs might take place. Thus, the Music Hall section had Music Hall #1, Music Hall #2, etc. And sometimes the songs were based upon some title or phrase I had given him before he left.

Harvey likes to travel. I like to stay at home. I like to get up at the same time each morning and eat the same thing and go to my desk and put out the paper and the pencil or pen, and then "begin." I make voyages similar to his, but I do mine at home. ("In my mind's eye, Horatio.") While he is amassing melodies, I am similarly putting down ideas for song lyrics, some taken from the source material, some of my own invention. Sometimes these lyrics are merely titles or fragments. Often they are complete. And just as Harvey may write several possibilities for a particular song or section, I will often write several lyrics or part-lyrics for the same spot.

During the course of this "separation," Harvey and I keep in touch. He sends me tapes of song melodies as he is composing, and I send him lyrics. And we continue to write back and forth about our impressions of the work—what seems strong, what seems weak, where we need to tighten up and where we need to expand. We begin to grope for the shape, the form, the put-together. I will, by this time, have come up with a clear and concise statement about the premise, and we will have talked about the "concept," the theatrical "signature" of the show. And we will constantly judge our new work by our increasing knowledge of the shape and meaning of the show we are hoping to write.

By the time we get back together, much of the score will be written and I will have done a basic blocking out of the script: what to trim, what to expand, what to cut completely. We will, from the very beginning, have jointly decided on the act break, where it should be and what it should be. And Harvey, since he is an artist, will have made some rough sketches of the stage as we envision it, and will have collected photographs and/or paintings to help fuel his imagination, and mine.

The next phase is like a miniature version of the first two. We meet together and then we split. We no longer do it in such an extreme form as going to different countries, but more often than not, I will journey from my home in Connecticut into New York for a couple of days, during which Harvey and I meet every afternoon, talking out problems, singing the songs and reading the scenes, frequently taping them so that we can both listen back in the privacy of our own spaces to try and make an objective judgment about what we have accomplished. Then we decide what needs to be done next, which of us does what, and we split for another week or ten days, until I return to New York or Harvey comes to Connecticut.

As we get further down the line, we prepare a "backer's audition," in which we perform a compressed version of the script and score. These are not necessarily for backers; at least, not at first. They are for trusted associates and friends. Then later for the producer or producers. Then for possible directors, then for backers, then for designers and orchestrators; and then, if all goes well, for principal actors or stars.

If you write plays, you type them and send them in and await your fate. If you write musicals, you perform them yourself. You stand face to face with fate (often in the form of a very cynical, very bored theater owner or Broadway "angel") and you watch their reactions as you try to make them weep or laugh. It is hard. Very hard. But it is a wonderful way to find out something about your show. If a tired Broadway-type never cracks a smile, or possibly dozes off, it may not mean too much, just as if your best friend or closest relative reacts with unrestrained emotion, it won't mean too much. But if you begin to get the same reaction over and over again with different kinds of people, that is something to pay attention to. If the same number consistently gets that big laugh and that surge of applause, don't cut it. On the other hand, if you get to a spot in the story or the score where you always feel "out on a limb," where you know you have to hurry forward to combat the growing restlessness, that is a clear and present danger signal and should be observed now, before the *merde* hits the fan in previews (or on opening night).

Finally, I have three books I would like to recommend if you are interested in learning more about the art and craft of lyric writing.

The first is one by Lehman Engel, *Their Words are Music*, published in 1975 by Crown. It covers sixteen lyricists from 1925 to 1972, studying each quite thoroughly in terms of technique and style. Then it has a section on the four lyricists who collaborated with Kurt Weill, comparing and contrasting their contributions. Next Engel selects one show-song from a show (On or Off-Broadway) for each year from 1920 to 1975. And last, he includes lyrics by twenty or so young writers who studied in his BMI Workshop, many of whom would go on to fame after this book was published, such as Ed Kleban (*A Chorus Line*), Alan Menken (*Little Shop of Horrors*, *Beauty and the Beast*), and Maury Yeston (*Nine*, *Grand Hotel*, *Titanic*). It is wonderful to have such a broad and diverse group of lyricists and lyrics, and especially to have them broken apart and dissected for detailed analysis. The only complaint I have about the book is that in the chapter about me, the picture above the caption "Tom Jones" is one of Harvey Schmidt, smiling seraphically as he poses in his tuxedo above a lionskin rug.

The two other books I would like to recommend for those interested in lyric writing are:

Lyrics by Oscar Hammerstein II, re-issued in 1985 by Hal Leonard Books, P.O. Box 13819, 8112 W. Bluemound Road, Milwaukee, WI 53213. This collection of Hammerstein lyrics has a foreword by Stephen Sondheim, a preface by Richard Rodgers, and a rather extensive "Notes On Lyrics" section by Hammerstein, speaking in an easy and conversational way about the put-together of lyrics.

Lyrics on Several Occasions, originally published in 1959, when Ira Gershwin was alive, and just reissued by Limelight Editions, 118 East 30th Street, New York, N. Y. 10016. This wide ranging collection of Gershwin's lyrics, with notations (and variations) by the writer, is probably the most fun of the books on my list, since it manages to provide a wealth of rather erudite information in a casual and amusing way.

11

Getting Produced

It's been my experience that whenever I speak with aspiring young musical theatre writers, the thing they most want to know is how a show actually manages to get produced. Even though they understand full well that no two cases are the same and that the environment for production is always changing, they have a great desire to find out the details of what actually took place during a specific show. With this in mind, I will briefly note some of my experiences, while stressing that these "case histories" are not only different from each other but also different from anything that will arise in the future. Each case is unique, and the things one learns from one experience will probably bear no relationship to what will happen the next time out.

In the case of *The Fantasticks* the turning point was a production in a summer theatre at Barnard College in New York City. After working unsuccessfully on a big Broadway version of the Rostand play *Les Romanesques* for several years, we threw it all out and wrote *The Fantasticks* in three weeks when our friend Word Baker said he could get us a production on a bill of-one acts he was directing at Barnard.

We had one week of rehearsal, followed by one week of performance. At our first run-through, our first time in the theatre, our talented young leading lady, Susan Watson, lost her voice. Not only that, she had fallen from a ladder and severely bruised her ribs. She couldn't sing. She couldn't dance. And though she could still speak, her hoarse voice could scarcely rise above a whisper. We decided that, for the purposes of the run-through, Harvey, at the piano, would sing her songs while she mouthed the words. Our choreographer would dance for her. After all, what did it matter? It was only a run-through.

Susan Watson and the Barnard cast of *The Fantasticks*. (The actor in the bowler hat is Ron Leibman; next to him, holding onto the pole, is Bill Tost, currently playing Ron's role at Sullivan Street thirty-eight years later.)

It was at this point that Lore Noto entered our lives. He arrived, uninvited and unannounced, along with his lawyer, Donald Farber, explaining that our director had told him he could drop in anytime. I was furious. I tried to tell him that this was our first run-through, that our leading lady was ill, that the show was not ready to be seen or judged, and that it would be better for all concerned if Mr. Noto took his lawyer and left, returning after the show had actually opened.

But Lore could not be moved. He was—and is—a very determined man. (That's one reason *The Fantasticks* has run so long.) So, with our director's blessing, he stayed and watched the entire show. What he saw was strange indeed. Every time the heroine began to sing, a heavy masculine voice with a decided Texas twang seemed to come from her mouth. Every time she started to dance, a young man in blue jeans stepped onstage and began to move in her place. Every time she spoke, it was in a whisper scarcely audible to the human ear.

Lore loved it. He thought it was brilliant. He said that he wanted to produce it. However, Harvey and I decided to wait before making a decision. After all, we hadn't really seen the show ourselves yet and we weren't sure what we had. Plus which, we didn't know what to make of this strange man with his white suit, his Panama hat, and his lawyer by his side. We thought that he was some sort of eccentric millionaire, which turned out to be only partly true. In actual fact, not only was Lore struggling along as an artist's representative, he subsequently quit his job and invested his life savings (three thousand dollars) to put *The Fantasticks* on.

When the week's run at Barnard was finished, we had two other offers from people who wanted to produce the show. One wanted to keep the one-act form and add our revue material to make a complete evening. Another wanted to turn it into a full-length musical, but refused to pay the five hundred dollar advance which Harvey and I decided we were entitled to demand. Finally, there was Lore, who wanted to make it full-length, would pay the advance, and, as a final inducement, offered to write into the contract that he would have no say about artistic matters unless Harvey, Word Baker, and I were hopelessly deadlocked. This testament of faith was the deciding factor and we chose Lore Noto as our producer, a decision we have never regretted.

Incidentally, the show, which was budgeted at a mere sixteen thousand, five hundred dollars, took eight months of continual backer's auditions to finance.

There are two things to be learned from this initial experience of ours. One: it makes the job of finding a producer much, much easier if you can get a staged production of your musical. It doesn't have to be the greatest production of all time. It doesn't have to run more than a few performances. But seeing a show live as opposed to reading a script and listening to a tape will help clarify what the show is about and, especially, how it plays in front of an audience. The other point is that, once you have been lucky enough to find a producer, it doesn't mean that you are on the way to immediate production. First the money must be raised, which will require a whole set of special skills on your part in the form of auditions, presentation tapes, and so forth.

After *The Fantasticks* opened, we were contacted by the producer of the hit musical *Bye, Bye, Birdie*, who said he admired our work and would like to do a show with us. Did we have any ideas? Well, we were interested in a novel called *Professor Fodorsky*, which we envisioned as a musical built around the drawings of Saul Steinberg. We told the producer about it, but explained that we had already spoken to Cheryl Crawford about the idea and we felt we were honor-bound to do the show with her. Two weeks later he had optioned the novel and assigned it to the "Birdie boys" to write (under the title *All American*). I probably don't have to point out the moral of this little story, but just in case: keep your mouth shut until you have an option! After that, still keep your mouth shut.

I mentioned in an earlier chapter how *110 in the Shade* came to be. It was brought to us by N. Richard Nash, the author of *The Rainmaker*, who had formed a partnership with David Merrick to produce a musical version. He had seen our work. He liked it. He offered us the chance. A similar thing happened with *I Do! I Do!* Gower Champion had been one of the most ardent champions of *The Fantasticks* in its early, struggling days. He said he would like to do a show with us. When an opportunity came along, he gave us a call.

Those two were easy. At least, they were easy to finance. Both were produced by David Merrick, and when David Merrick decided to produce something, it got produced. The backers were there. The theatres were available. The theatre-party agents were ready to sign up, as were the record album companies. Merrick's huge and efficient production organization, involving the casting people, the publicity staff, stage managers, and so forth, simply started to roll. After all, he was doing five or six Broadway shows every year, at least half of them musicals.

The other dark side of the story—wild outbursts, frequent, almost operatic, explosions of rage, the use of cruelty and intimidation as a method of coercion—was the price you paid for all the financing and efficiency. And in that sense, no show with Merrick could ever be called easy.

Celebration had been promised to Cheryl Crawford for years before it was even written. The money was raised after a week of invited performances at our Portfolio studio. This was before the era of "workshop productions," by the way. There were no rules to guide us, and no restrictions. Later, after the enormous success of *A Chorus Line*, which was created in a workshop, there were all manner of rules and regulations devised to protect the actors, and others, from being exploited. After all, if they had helped to "create" the piece, they deserved a "piece" of the piece.

As time went on, the entire status of these so-called "workshop productions" became more and more and confused. The circumstances of *A Chorus Line,* using events and "dialogue" from the dancers' own lives, made for a rather special occasion. Few directors or writers knew how to use a theatre company to "create" a piece, as The Open Theatre and The Living Theatre had done in the 60's and *A Chorus Line* did in the 70's. Most writers did not want actors creating the show in the first place. Nevertheless, workshopping became the fashion of the day. Expensive as it was, it was still cheaper than taking a new musical out of town.

The end result in many cases was that producers of new musicals used workshops as elaborate backers' auditions.

Here is how it worked: Enough money was raised to assemble a creative team, cast the show, hire a few musicians, and rent a rehearsal space. Rehearsals were conducted for three or four weeks with director, conductor, and choreographer handling their usual assignments in the usual way. Very rarely did the actors actually "improvise." Almost never did they contribute lines and help create characters or situations. They did what a company does. They learned the material. They brought it to life as best they could. Then they did a series of workshop performances, without costumes or sets, for theatre owners, backers, and other theatrical professionals.

If the show created enough excitement, it moved on to full production. If it didn't, it didn't. If there was enough hope (and money), another workshop might be scheduled after the show was rewritten.

It was a way of trying to "hedge the bet," to offer some insurance against the enormous cost of producing a modern musical on Broadway. The actors were paid, but not much. And there is no doubt (in my mind) that they deserved (and deserve) to be fully compensated for their efforts and to be offered their roles if the show goes on.

On the other hand, I do feel that, because of the misleading example of *A Chorus Line* (and *Dreamgirls* and *Nine* and one or two others), writers often found themselves contractually responsible for compensating actors for things which the actors did not actually do. In the example I outlined above, where the workshop is really a try-out, with no unusual script or creative contributions by the cast, the author is nevertheless obliged to pay them a percentage of all future royalties, just as if they had contributed story and dialogue, as happened in *A Chorus Line*.

My own advice would be to avoid the workshop contract unless you have a show that is actually going to be substantially created in the workshop environment. If your script and score are basically complete before rehearsals, I would strongly suggest that, instead of a workshop, you:

1. Find a production somewhere, in a regional theatre, a summer theatre, a college, or a community theatre. Then use this production both as a place to rewrite and as an opportunity to invite potential producers and/or investors.

2. Go into a production with a showcase contract at one of the many theatres in New York (and elsewhere) which operate under such a contract. The advantage is that you don't have to sign your life away. The disadvantage is that you won't have much time to rewrite or try out new ideas, especially after the show has opened.
3. Do a staged reading of your show. Either set it up on your own or seek out one of the theatre groups that specialize in such events. Try to generate enough interest to move on to (1) or (2) above.
4. Get into a training program such as the ones operated by ASCAP or BMI or the Dramatists Guild, where arrangements are made to have your work performed by professionals and critiqued by experts. You can use this to learn more about your show, what to rewrite, etc., and as a stepping stone to (3) above so you can eventually advance to (1) or (2).

If you have a producer who wants to do a workshop production of your musical, and is willing to put up the considerable amount of money involved, you should probably take him or her up on it. But check your contracts. And try to see if your producer has any contact with regional theatres where the show might be done instead.

As for Harvey and me, we are in much the same position as the rest of the world. Gone are the days when a simple phone call from Gower Champion or Richard Nash could set a Broadway musical in motion. Actually, it was never *that* easy. In the case of *I Do! I Do!*, even with Gower Champion and David Merrick, Mary Martin turned us down once and Robert Preston five times over a period of two years before we actually got them to sign on for the show.

(One wild but true story: after Mary signed her contract, she went to her ranch in Brazil with her husband, Richard Halliday. They had no phone, no mail service, not even any electricity. When Bob Preston held back and Gower wanted to suggest another star, he had to send his assistant, Lucia Victor, to Brazil for the answer. First she flew to Rio. Then she took a commuter plane to Brasilia, in the center of the country. Then she went by bus to a small town called Annapolis and finally by jeep through the jungle to Mary and Richard's ranch. Having done all that, she told Mary the name of the actor we had in mind. Mary said "No," and Lucia turned around and came back.)

At this point in our careers. Harvey and I have the advantage of some name recognition, but that can be a curse as well as a blessing. Producers are often looking for new writers, new ideas, new blood. When you are starting out, no one knows your limitations. Anything seems possible. Who knows? Maybe you're the next Lloyd Webber or Stephen Sondheim or Jonathan Larson. If you can get one piece on, and it's well received, producers will be after you by the dozens.

With our most recent works, Harvey and I have been lucky enough to find encouragement and support from a variety of sources. *Grover's Corners*, our musical version of *Our Town* was, in effect, "tried out" by the National Alliance for Musical Theatre, a conglomerate of producers from around the country who have set out to encourage new musicals which might play in their theatres. Our newest show, *Mirette*, with score by us and libretto by Elizabeth Diggs, was developed at the Sundance Playwrights Unit and later fully staged at the wonderful Norma Terrace Theatre at Goodspeed, in Chester, Connecticut. One of our recent works was done at the York Theatre; and another by Musical Theatre Works, both "showcase" theatres in New York.

The new piece, *Mirette*, with a book by Elizabeth Diggs, tried out at Goodspeed at Chester.

As for the future, it is impossible to predict. The old way of doing Broadway musicals has changed. Almost none of them are actually created on Broadway anymore. They come from regional theatres (in and out of New York), from workshops, from small experimental spaces Off-Broadway. The only thing that hasn't changed is that getting started will be largely up to you. You won't find an agent, you won't find a producer, you won't find a production until you yourself can somehow get your musical performed somewhere where it can be heard.

For that reason, I strongly urge you to get as much general training in all aspects of theatre as possible, rather than limiting yourself to one area such as composing, writing lyrics, etc. Getting the show on will very likely depend on you, especially the first time. It will help a lot if you know how it's done.

POSTSCRIPT

A BRIEF SUMMARY AND A GARLAND OF PRECEPTS

I.

It seems to me that the American musical is sprung from two basic sources:

The first is "Variety." Pure entertainment. Directly influenced by the American minstrel show, but tracing its roots to ancient times and weaving down through the centuries (see Allardyce Nicoll's *Masks, Mimes, and Miracles*), this is the "fun" part that has traditionally been a key element in the popularity of the American musical comedy. In this tradition, plots are not that important. Neither are characters. Performers are important. Tunes are important. And snappy dances. And girls. And gags. And change of pace.

The second source is the theatre itself, with the theatre's values. That is to say, the value of story and character—of unified style. The major trend in American musicals for the last fifty years has been on increased effort to fuse traditional theatrical values with the variety-oriented musical comedy.

Even a writer such as Sondheim, although eager to explore new territory and to stretch the boundaries of the musical form, was careful to include the comedy numbers and the change-of-pace "variety" in his early shows. Tutored by Oscar Hammerstein II, working with Jerome Robbins, who himself had been tutored by George Abbott, he took it for granted that a musical, however serious its intentions, must find a place for those traditional crowd-pleasing elements.

Indeed, almost all of the notable American musical theatre writers of the past few decades have come under the direct influence of this traditional musical comedy heritage. Kander and Ebb were influenced by Bob Fosse as well as by Hal Prince, both of whom were influenced by George Abbott. Cy Coleman got his initiation with Bob Fosse; Jerry Herman with Gower Champion; Bock and Harnick with Abbott, Robbins, and Prince. Of course, as I have stated many times, all of the above were influenced by Rodgers and Hammerstein, who always made sure to have plenty of the old musical comedy know-how in their book-oriented shows.

The question is: What happens next? What happens as these writers and directors who carried on the old musical comedy traditions pass the torch to the next generation? Sondheim represents the major influence on most of the young writers now. And though he himself is a past master of these traditional entertainment forms, his inclination seems increasingly to take him further away from "showbiz" and ever deeper into serious works more concerned with depth and style than with crowd-pleasing "variety." Where he leads, I think the others are bound to follow.

But I think there is a danger. Just as the early musicals were doomed like dinosaurs by their casual disregard for plot and character, I think it is quite possible that these new, more serious musicals may find themselves doomed by their heaviness, by their neglect of the verities of vaudeville.

Finding the right balance—that is the secret. I have a wonderful cartoon from *The New Yorker* on the wall just above my desk. In it, a novelist sits gazing thoughtfully at his typewriter. Above him, on either side, are two tiny apparitions. One, with its head ringed by a halo, is saying: "A historical novel packed with plausible, motivated characters who epitomize man's constant struggle for goodness and purpose in a brutal and morally bankrupt society." The other apparition, horns on head, says simply: "Tits and ass!" And that about sums it up.

II.

Looking at the development of the musical over the past century since its birth, the most striking single feature to me is the steadily shrinking volume of production.

Once there were lots of musicals. Now there are few. Soon, presumably, there will be fewer. Look at the young Jerome Kern. He contributed to twenty-four shows in three years. Every composer and lyricist did at least one new show a year. Most did two. Many did three or more. I am speaking not just of revues, but of complete scores.

Now look at the last few years. Look at the Tony nominations. Sometimes they can't even come up with a single musical to nominate for best book. Sometimes shows that were disasters, shows that ran for one week, are nominated simply to have four names to provide some semblance of competition.

Of course, part of this may be the result of competition from other forms of entertainment such as television, films, records, etc. But hold on. There aren't any musicals on television. Not even any musical variety shows any more. There aren't many film musicals either. Musicals belong to the stage. Check weekly *Variety*. Read the grosses. Eighty percent of the money made on Broadway is made by the musicals. The percentage is even higher on the road. If you visit New York from out of town, what do you want to see? A musical. Maybe two.

So—what happened? Why are there so few new musicals?

In a curious way, the popularity of musicals has helped to contribute to their demise. Somewhere along the line, probably around the time of Rodgers and Hammerstein, musicals became the big moneymakers of Broadway. More than that, musicals became the hot ticket, the thing to see. It was hard to get a ticket to *South Pacific*. But everybody had to see it. (Musicals began to have the first huge advance sales in history, a key factor in this process.) People would pay anything to see *South Pacific*. Even ordinary people. Expense account people would pay *more* than anything to see it. They would pay double anything!

At some point, with the success and the scalpers and the advance sales and the new phenomenon of theatre parties, actually seeing the show became only part of the experience. The other part (for many people, the most important part) was being able to say you had seen the show. It became a status symbol. It became something other than just going to a show for enjoyment. There was a mysticism about it, as if, by being one of the lucky few to participate in the show's enormous success, some of the magic would rub off on you.

And so, the megahit was born. And with it, a vicious circle began: a circle which has been spiraling inward and downward ever since, imploding, like a black hole. A megahit meant that money was made by the millions. A true megahit was, and is, like a money-printing machine for everyone involved: writers, producers, directors, stars, theatre owners. What do you think Andrew Lloyd Webber makes a week at this moment? Two hundred and fifty thousand dollars? (A million a month?) I'd say more. Much more.

But wait, what about the stagehands? What about the musicians? What about the chorus kids, and the dressers, and the publicity people? If millions were being made, why shouldn't they get their share? Thus, new contracts were negotiated, contracts based on the concept of megahits, contracts which, in time, effectively killed off any marginal shows, which might have survived in another era.

Another result: With a megahit, there was enormous money to be made. Therefore, you had to gamble millions in order to possibly make tens of millions, twenties of millions. And hey, if you have a megahit, you could raise the prices. Forty, fifty, sixty—soon maybe a hundred dollars a ticket. Of course, at these prices, people won't go to the theatre as a regular practice. It won't become a habit, not at three or four hundred bucks for an evening out.

And if it costs that much to go to the theatre, you don't want to just see a show. You've got to see something special. Something spectacular. For that kind of dough, you want to see some scenery, some costumes, some special effects. You want to see some roller skating, or a huge tire that ascends into the ceiling, or a chandelier that falls (almost) into the audience. In short, you want to see where your money went.

And so it goes, in a vicious circle.

Hits make more money, so things cost more money. Things cost more money, so ticket prices go up and people go less often. People go less often, so fewer shows get done. Fewer shows get done, so fewer writers get a chance. Fewer of musical theatre gets reduced to a mere handful of creative artists. And since they are proven moneymakers, they are expensive. And since they are expensive, shows cost more. Etc., etc., etc.

III.

What will happen? No one knows. But I do have some thoughts about it, thoughts which will not be new to you if you have read the preceding chapters.

I think the musical theatre will survive—perhaps even thrive. And I don't just mean the boffola Broadway mega-hits and the extravaganzas. No. I mean the musicals of more or less human scale which can be done by people, for people, in a rather ancient and primitive (and inexpensive) way. I think the "lyric" theatre, the "open" theatre, the "presentational" theatre will survive, and I think the musical theatre will survive because it is a vital part of that lyric theatre.

There is a hunger for this ancient theatre. I have seen it at work. *The Fantasticks* has survived, and thrived, not because of its original or brilliant story, or because of the uniqueness or depth of its characters, or even because of the beauty of its music. It has survived because it has given the audience something they hunger for and can't easily get elsewhere. They are part of the show. They help to create it. They have an experience which is ancient, and basic, and which cannot be duplicated either by television or film.

A Garland of Precepts

1. Finding the Form.

Somebody famous (I think it was Voltaire) once said: "Everybody is smarter than anybody," and I think that is true. You have only to work on a few musicals to discover that, no matter how experienced the creators may be, they don't really know what they have until the audience tells them.

I would go further and paraphrase that remark by adding that, when working in musical theatre, "Everything is more important than anything." The overall shape, the "breathing" in and out, the balance between small and large, between realistic and presentational—the shape of the forest, so to speak —is more important than any of the trees.

If you want to create musicals, this is the most important (and most mysterious) thing to learn: the shape, the form, the "everything." Try to become aware of it. Try to learn to sense it, to "feel" it, for it is something that cannot be taught; it can only be acquired.

How do you go through that initiation? How do you acquire this awareness? There is only one way. By personal experience. Only if you have seen hundreds of shows, and I mean really *seen* them—heard them, been around them, been in them, been a part of them in some way—will some of this knowledge miraculously seep in.

And then, only if a fair percentage of these shows are classics will the initiation have any merit at all. To be around endless sitcoms is to take on the thinking and, worse, the rhythms of endless sitcoms. That's fine; if you want to write endless sitcoms. It pays well, and your family will be reassured. But I must tell you: Life is short. And there is no such thing as real security, anyway. There exists another kind of drama, the drama of Shakespeare, for example, and of *Porgy and Bess* and *My Fair Lady* and *Jesus Christ, Superstar* and *Sweeney Todd* and *Guys and Dolls*. These things, too, can seep into your subconscious, can offer an initiation. And these things, too, can nourish you.

Sitcoms (and among those I would include many well-made musicals) can provide you with "bread," but they can't nourish you. Of all the many plays that I was involved with in college, and there were hundreds of them, the plays of Shakespeare were the most nutritious. I didn't know it at the time, but later I found that I remembered them. I remembered certain speeches. I remembered certain "moods." I remembered certain silences, certain crowd scenes followed by certain solo turns.

If you want to really learn something about form and construction for the musical theatre, take a couple of Shakespeare's plays and study them, really study them. Break them apart. Lay them out in an outline. (Remembering that in the actual theatre of his time there were no act breaks, no scene changes, none of the editorial nonsense that was added to the scripts in the nineteenth century.) Lay out the plays and look for: (a) how many "scenes" there are; (b) what variations there are in the size of scenes; (c) what the function is of each scene in the entire structure; (d) what is the "variety," the interplay between "light" and "dark" scenes; and (e) how many solo "arias" there are and where.

You will find, among other things, enormous variety, change of pace, enormous "flow." Plus which, if you really study the plays of Shakespeare, you will find that each actor in the company gets at least one good bit in every show, a chance to shine. You will also find that the star parts are given a rest period offstage before their biggest and most demanding scenes, a chance to go to the bathroom, or get a drink of water, or simply to think and get ready.

If you do all of this in outline form, you will be very impressed. And you will learn a lot. But if you want to love the plays, be around them in performance. That's when they will "enter" you. That's when they will "inform" you.

2. Learn By Copying.

Of course, simply studying Shakespeare is not sufficient training for the musical theatre. You must study the great musicals as well. And, having studied them, I would suggest you "ape" them, copy them. If you are a lyricist you should deliberately try to write something in the style of the great Mr. Gilbert. Then immerse yourself in the clever and modish rhyming of Cole Porter. I remember my own learning days, listening to endless Porter albums and coming up with what I thought were brilliant rhyme patterns. For example, this scrap of lyric from a song entitled "If You Want to Live in Sin (Don't Get a Cold-water Flat"):

> I know that bed-opus
> That made Oed-opus
> A Rex...

Believe me, there were worse ones than this. I blush to dig them out of the files, much less put them in a book for people to read, but hopefully they will make the point that early efforts may be hopelessly sophomoric and self-conscious yet still be part of a valuable training.

Read the lyrics of the great show writers. Listen to their albums. Copy their work. Then (and only then), forget it. Find your own voice. Don't seek to find it; just let it happen. Find the things that you like, the things that turn you on, that move you to laughter or to tears. And then embrace them. And write them. Find out how to put down on paper the things that you feel, the impressions that you have.

Let me stress one more time: Just as when studying, you should concentrate on the great classics, when you are copying, you should copy only the best. In particular, copy the great classics of the past. The sources of your own time are already all around you. They are influencing you, anyway. Don't just copy Stephen Sondheim, for example. For when you look around, you will see that is what everyone else is doing.

3. Write "hot."

Colette once said: "It is neither advisable nor wise to conceive a child with too much thought." And it is the same with art. You need to know where you are going when you write. You need to know "what it is about." You need to know, in general terms, the plot, and to have strong feelings about the characters. And then, you need to—"cast off"—to write free. To go wild. To let your wrist, your fingers, lead you.

Don't stop. Don't ever stop in the process and think: "But wait, this isn't what I planned." It's like love-making. You know the general objective, but you have to let the passion of the moment guide you, lead you, establish the rhythms, and the variations of the rhythms. When it works well, there is a kind of mood that takes over, almost like a trance or a heightened state, in which things happen seemingly beyond your mental self. This is as true in writing as it is in love-making.

Then comes the disillusionment of the next morning, at least in writing (and sometimes in love-making, too). There is a bitter saying that the women have along the border towns of Mexico: "Last night you called me senorita; today you call me dirty Mexican." It's like that with the writing, sometimes. "Last night you called me masterpiece; today you call me turgid prose."

How does one get such "passion" to happen when one is writing? Paradoxically, it comes by planning and hard work, by "plugging away," by strict routine. You never wait for it, not if you are a professional. You plug away on a regular basis. And when it comes, it comes. It will take over (briefly) and then disappear. And then you resume plugging away until it comes again.

If it never comes, if your "hand" never takes over from your brain, and creates so furiously that you feel that it will fall off, then I question whether you are really a writer.

4. You Are What You Eat.

You are no more than you are. You perceive no more than you perceive. You feel no more than you feel. And you can only create from the reservoir of what you yourself are.

Expose yourself to many things.

Be curious. Be curious about history, about knowledge, most of all, about people. Be curious about yourself. Explore.

Feel many things. Don't protect yourself. Don't thicken your skin. No matter how painful it becomes, don't play safe with your feelings.

Life, as I said, is short. You may experience it and pay the price. Or you may play it safe and reduce the risks. It's up to you. One thing you can't do is only feel the good. So many people want that. So many people try for it. But of course, it is impossible. Your ability to feel is your ability to feel. To the exact degree that you are capable of feeling pleasure—to that exact same degree, you will feel pain.

Many people, finding the painful parts of life too terrible to bear, simply anesthetize their feelings. They sink into a dim, half-world of muted sensations. Not Colette. That's one reason that I love her. She knew the secret. When asked in her advanced old age, if she could look back over her life and keep part of it and throw part of it away, what would she keep and what would she throw away, she replied: "I'd keep it all! It's my property! My goods!"

The advice I give to you is the same that I give myself: Don't be afraid. Open yourself up. Learn to accept, and even to relish, the bad as well as the good, the pain as well as the pleasure. Of course, I don't pretend that I am always courageous enough to follow my own advice.

5. Be Idealistic.

This is a tough business, a cruel business. The competition, especially in New York and especially in the musical theatre, is fierce. Not without reason is there the saying: "It's not enough that I succeed, my friends have to also fail." There is a tendency after you have been in the rat race for a while to open the *Times* and slowly relish the roasting given to some competitor, possibly even to some friend.

You must have something to hold on to, some form of belief in the value of what you are doing. Otherwise, you are a loser. Even if you "win," you will still be a loser. And you will know it.

When I graduated from college, I had a dream of belonging to a new theatre, a theatre which I, and others like me, would create. This was before the establishment of the marvelous network of regional theatres across the country. It was before the grants and the endowments. It was even before Off-Broadway had established itself as an alternative place to create. In short, there were no role models and I didn't know what to do.

As on many other occasions when I needed counsel, I sought out my mentor, the distinguished director and teacher, B. Iden Payne. I explained my dilemma to him and he listened very carefully. Then, speaking in dead earnest (in his muted British accent), he gave me the following advice.

I should (he said) gather together my group and be sure that we were all equally well-trained and committed to our ideals of a new theatre. Then we should write down on placards and banners who we were and what it was we wanted, and we should march. We should start in Times Square in New York City, and we should beat a drum and march against the oncoming traffic.

"You will probably manage to get a block or so the first time before you get arrested," he said. "And they won't throw you in jail. They will simply ask you to promise not to do it again and, of course, you will agree. Then, as soon as you are released, you must go back to the exact same place where you were stopped and you must begin marching again. And beating your drum.

"This time you will be arrested. But not for long. One or two nights, at most. They will again make you promise not to disturb the peace, and again you will promise. But when you get out of jail, you must go back to the place where you were arrested and you must start marching all over again. Keep this up over and over, no matter how long it takes, and I promise that eventually someone will believe in you and will help you start your theatre."

Now, you have to understand that this advice was given in the early 1950's, long before the days of protests and marches and banners and such. It caught me totally by surprise and it inspired me, even though I knew it was a most unlikely scenario. For he was saying that if you want something enough, if you believe in it enough, if you dare enough, people will respond and they will help you. He was saying that faith has enormous power; that it can, in fact, move mountains.

I never had the courage to march. Maybe some of you will. In any case, good luck. I wish you the very, very best. And maybe I can at least loan you a drum.